# Ruby on Rails
*Up and Running*

# Other resources from O'Reilly

# Ruby on Rails
*Up and Running*

*Bruce A. Tate and Curt Hibbs*

O'REILLY®

Beijing · Cambridge · Farnham · Köln · Paris · Sebastopol · Taipei · Tokyo

**Ruby on Rails: Up and Running**
by Bruce A. Tate and Curt Hibbs

Published by O'Reilly Media, Inc., 1005 Gravenstein Highway North, Sebastopol, CA 95472.

O'Reilly books may be purchased for educational, business, or sales promotional use. Online editions are also available for most titles (*safari.oreilly.com*). For more information, contact our corporate/institutional sales department: (800) 998-9938 or *corporate@oreilly.com*.

| | |
|---|---|
| **Editor:** Mike Loukides | **Indexer:** John Bicklehaupt |
| **Production Editor:** Adam Witwer | **Cover Designer:** Karen Montgomery |
| **Copyeditor:** Nancy Kotary | **Interior Designer:** David Futato |
| **Proofreader:** Mary Anne Weeks Mayo | **Illustrators:** Robert Romano and Jessamyn Read |

**Printing History:**

| | |
|---|---|
| August 2006: | First Edition. |

RepKover™ This book uses RepKover™, a durable and flexible lay-flat binding.

ISBN-13: 978-0-596-10132-9 | ISBN-10: 0-596-10132-5
[M]

# Table of Contents

# Preface

The Ruby on Rails phenomenon is sweeping through our industry with reckless disregard for established programming languages, longstanding conventions, or commercial support. You can get a whole lot of information on Ruby on Rails from articles on the Web, excellent books, and even formal coursework. However, there's something missing. How does an established programmer, armed with nothing more than a little Ruby knowledge, go just beyond the basics, and be productive in Rails?

With *Ruby on Rails: Up and Running*, we are not going to reiterate the reference manual or replace Google. Instead, we'll strive to give you the big picture of how Rails applications hold together and tell you where to go for the information that we don't cover in the chapters. You will see how Rails dynamically adds features to all database models, called Active Record objects. By understanding the big picture, you'll be able to make better use of the best reference manuals to fill in the details.

We won't try to make you digest a whole lot of words. Instead, we'll give you the theory in the context of an end-to-end application. We'll walk you through the creation of a simple project—one that is a little more demanding than a blog or shopping cart, but with a simple enough structure that a Rails beginner will be able to quickly understand what's going on.

We're not going to try to cover each new feature. Instead, we'll show you the ones we see as the backbone, forming the most important elements to understand. We will also cover migrations and Ajax in some detail, because you won't find too much information on those two frameworks yet.

In short, we're not trying to build a comprehensive Rails library. We're going to give you the foundation you need to get up and running.

## Who Should Read This Book?

*Ruby on Rails: Up and Running* is for experienced developers who are new to Rails and possibly to Ruby. To use this book, you don't have to be a strong Ruby programmer. We do expect you to be a programmer, though. You should know enough about your chosen platform to be able to write programs, install software, run scripts using the system console, edit files, use a database, and understand how basic web applications work.

## Conventions Used in This Book

The following typographic conventions are used in this book:

Plain text

> Indicates menu titles, menu options, menu buttons, and keyboard accelerators (such as Alt and Ctrl).

*Italic*

> Indicates new terms, URLs, email addresses, filenames, file extensions, pathnames, directories, and Unix utilities.

`Constant width`

> Indicates commands, the contents of files, and the output from commands.

**`Constant width bold`**

> Shows commands or other text that should be typed literally by the user.

*`Constant width italic`*

> Shows text that should be replaced with user-supplied values.

 This icon signifies a tip, suggestion, or general note.

 This icon indicates a warning or caution.

## Using Code Examples

This book is here to help you get your job done. In general, you may use the code in this book in your programs and documentation. You do not need to contact us for permission unless you're reproducing a significant portion of the code. For example, writing a program that uses several chunks of code from this book does not require permission. Selling or distributing a CD-ROM of examples from O'Reilly books *does* require permission. Answering a question by citing this book and quoting example code does not require permission. Incorporating a significant amount of example code from this book into your product's documentation *does* require permission.

You can get sample code at the main page for *Ruby on Rails: Up and Running*: *http://www.oreilly.com/catalog/rubyrails/*. You will find a ZIP file that contains the sample project as it exists after each chapter, with each instance of the sample application numbered by chapter. If you want to skip a chapter, just download the right ZIP file.

We appreciate, but do not require, attribution. An attribution usually includes the title, author, publisher, and ISBN. For example: "*Ruby on Rails: Up and Running* by Bruce A. Tate and Curt Hibbs. Copyright 2006 O'Reilly Media, Inc., 978-0-596-10132-9."

If you feel that your use of code examples falls outside fair use or the permission given here, feel free to contact us at *permissions@oreilly.com*.

# Platforms

Ruby on Rails is cross-platform, but Unix and Windows shells behave differently. For consistency, we use Windows throughout the book. You can easily run the examples on the Unix or Mac OS X operating systems as well. You'll see a couple of minor differences:

- On Windows, you can specify paths with either the forward slash (/) or back-slash (\) character. We'll try to be consistent and use the forward slash to specify all paths.

- On Windows, to run the various Ruby scripts that make up Rails, you need to explicitly type ruby. On Unix environments, you don't. If you're running Unix, and you are instructed to type the command ruby script/server, feel free to omit the ruby.

- On Windows, to run a process in a separate shell, precede the command with start. On Unix and Mac OS X, append an ampersand (&) character to run the command in the background.

# Safari® Enabled

 When you see a Safari® Enabled icon on the cover of your favorite technology book, that means the book is available online through the O'Reilly Network Safari Bookshelf.

Safari offers a solution that's better than e-books. It's a virtual library that lets you easily search thousands of top tech books, cut and paste code samples, download chapters, and find quick answers when you need the most accurate, current information. Try it for free at *http://safari.oreilly.com*.

# How to Contact Us

We have tested and verified the information in this book and in the source code to the best of our ability, but given the amount of text and the rapid evolution of technology, you may find that features have changed or that we have made mistakes. If so, please notify us by writing to:

O'Reilly Media, Inc.
1005 Gravenstein Highway North
Sebastopol, CA 95472
800-998-9938 (in the United States or Canada)
707-829-0515 (international or local)
707-829-0104 (fax)

You can also send messages electronically. To be put on the mailing list or request a catalog, send email to:

*info@oreilly.com*

To ask technical questions or comment on the book, send email to:

*bookquestions@oreilly.com*

As mentioned in the earlier section, we have a web site for this book where you can find code, errata (previously reported errors and corrections available for public view), and other book information. You can access this web site at:

*http://www.oreilly.com/catalog/rubyrails*

For more information about this book and others, see the O'Reilly web site:

*http://www.oreilly.com*

# Acknowledgments

Writing a book is a demanding exercise, taking passion, commitment, and persistence. The authors on the cover get all of the glory (and possibly the blame). Many people contribute to a book. We'd like to mention the people who made writing this book such a fulfilling experience.

Collectively, Curt and Bruce would like to thank the outstanding team of reviewers who provided so many great comments, including David Mabelle, Mauro Cicio, Brooke Hedrick, Faisal Jawdat, Shane Claussen, Leo de Blaauw, Anne Bowman, Seth Havermann, Dave Hastings, and Randy Hanford. We'd also like to thank David Geary for fleshing out some of the early ideas in Photo Share.

*Ruby on Rails: Up and Running* would be nothing without the excellent contributions of the core Ruby on Rails team. We would like to thank David Heinemeier Hansson (the creator of Rails), Florian Weber, Jamis Buck, Jeremy Kemper, Leon Breedt, Marcel Molina, Jr., Michael Koziarski, Nicholas Seckar, Sam Stephenson, Scott Barron, Thomas Fuchs, and Tobias Luetke. Ruby is a fantastic language, and we would like to thank the many who made it so. We throw out specific thanks to Yukihiro Matsumoto (a.k.a. "Matz"), the creator of Ruby, and to Dave Thomas and

Andy Hunt, without whom Ruby might have remained virtually unknown outside of Japan.

Bruce would like to specifically thank Curt, for stepping into this project after it seemed that it was dead. Also, thanks to those at AutoGas who were so instrumental in trying this technology within the context of a real production application—especially the core development team, including Mathew Varghese, Karl Hoenshel, Cheri Byerley, Chris Gindorf, and Colby Blaisdell. Their collective experience shaped this book more than you will ever know. Thanks to my Dutch friend Leo, again, for being such a supportive influence on this book, though you're mostly a Java developer. You have had more influence on me than you might expect. More than anyone else, I would like to thank my family. Kayla and Julia, you are the sparks in my soul that keep the creative fires burning. Maggie, you are my inspiration, and I love you more than I can ever say.

Curt would like to thank his wife, Wasana, for letting him disappear behind his computer screen late into the night (and sometimes into the following day) without complaint. I would also like to thank my friends at O'Reilly, for giving me a forum to spread the word about the incredible productivity advantages of Ruby on Rails. Specifically, I'd like to thank chromatic for publishing my ONLamp.com articles, and Mike Loukides for not giving up when I kept telling him I didn't want to write a book.

# CHAPTER 1

# Zero to Sixty: Introducing Rails

Rails may just be the most important open source project to be introduced in the past 10 years. It's promoted as one of the most productive web development frameworks of all time and is based on the increasingly important Ruby programming language. What has happened so far?

- By December 2006, you're likely to see more published books on Rails than any of Java's single flagship frameworks, including JSF, Spring, or Hibernate.

- The Rails framework has been downloaded at least 500,000 times in only its second year, as of May 2006. These statistics compare favorably with the most popular open source frameworks in any language.*

- The Rails community mailing lists get hundreds of notes a day, compared to dozens on the most popular web development frameworks in other languages.

- The Rails framework has caused an explosion in the use of the Ruby programming language, which has been relatively obscure until recently.

- The Rails buzz generates increasingly hot debates on portals that focus on other programming languages. The Java community in particular has fiercely debated the Rails platform.

You don't have to go far to find great overviews of Rails. You can watch several educational videos that show Rails in action, narrated by the founder David Heinemeier Hansson. You can watch him build simple working applications, complete with a backing database and validation, in less than 10 minutes. But unlike the many quick-and-dirty environments you've seen, Rails lets you keep the quick and leave the dirty behind. It lets you build clean applications based on the model-view-controller philosophy. Rails is a special framework.

---

* The number 500,000 is actually a conservative estimate. Download statistics for a popular delivery vehicle, called *gems*, make it easy to track the number of Rails distributions by gems, but many other distributions exist, such as the Locomotive distribution on Mac OS X. The real download statistics could easily be twice this number.

Sure, Rails has its limitations. Ruby has poor support for object-relational mapping (ORM) for legacy schemas; the Rails approach is less powerful than Java's approach, for example.* Ruby does not yet have flagship integrated development environments. Every framework has limitations, and Rails is no different. But for a wide range of applications, the strengths of Rails far outpace its weaknesses.

## Rails Strengths

As you go through this book, you'll learn how Rails can thrive without all of the extensive libraries required by other languages. Ruby's flexibility lets you extend your applications in ways that might have been previously unavailable to you. You'll be able to use a Rails feature called *scaffolding* to put database-backed user interfaces in front of your customers quickly. Then, as you improve your code, the scaffolding melts away. You'll be able to build database-backed model objects with just a couple of lines of code, and Rails will fill in the tedious details.

The most common programming problem in today's typical development project involves building a web-based user interface to manage a relational database. For that class of problems, Rails is much more productive than any other web development framework either of us has ever used. The strengths aren't limited to any single groundbreaking invention; rather, Rails is packed with features that make you more productive, with many of the following features building on one other:

*Metaprogramming*
> Metaprogramming techniques use programs to write programs. Other frameworks use extensive code generation, which gives users a one-time productivity boost but little else, and customization scripts let the user add customization code in only a small number of carefully selected points. Metaprogramming replaces these two primitive techniques and eliminates their disadvantages. Ruby is one of the best languages for metaprogramming, and Rails uses this capability well.†

*Active Record*
> Rails introduces the Active Record framework, which saves objects to the database. Based on a design pattern cataloged by Martin Fowler, the Rails version of Active Record discovers the columns in a database schema and automatically attaches them to your domain objects using metaprogramming. This approach to wrapping database tables is simple, elegant, and powerful.

---

* For example, Hibernate supports three kinds of inheritance mapping, but Rails supports only single-table inheritance. Hibernate supports composite keys, but Rails is much more limited.

† Rails also uses code generation but relies much more on metaprogramming for the heavy lifting.

*Convention over configuration*

Most web development frameworks for .NET or Java force you to write pages of configuration code. If you follow suggested naming conventions, Rails doesn't need much configuration. In fact, you can often cut your total configuration code by a factor of five or more over similar Java frameworks just by following common conventions.

*Scaffolding*

You often create temporary code in the early stages of development to help get an application up quickly and see how major components work together. Rails automatically creates much of the scaffolding you'll need.

*Built-in testing*

Rails creates simple automated tests you can then extend. Rails also provides supporting code called *harnesses* and *fixtures* that make test cases easier to write and run. Ruby can then execute all your automated tests with the rake utility.

*Three environments: development, testing, and production*

Rails gives you three default environments: development, testing, and production. Each behaves slightly differently, making your entire software development cycle easier. For example, Rails creates a fresh copy of the Test database for each test run.

There's much more, too, including Ajax for rich user interfaces, partial views and helpers for reusing view code, built-in caching, a mailing framework, and web services. We can't get to all of Rails' features in this book; however, we will let you know where to get more information. But the best way to appreciate Rails is to see it in action, so let's get to it.

## Putting Rails into Action

You could manually install all of the components for Rails, but Ruby has something called *gems*. The gem installer accesses a web site, Ruby Forge, and downloads an application unit, called a gem, and all its dependencies. You can install Rails through gems, requesting all dependencies, with this command:[*]

```
gem install rails --include-dependencies
```

That's it—Rails is installed. There's one caveat: you also need to install the database support for your given database. If you've already installed MySQL, you're done. If

---

[*] If you want to code along with us, make sure you've installed Ruby and gems. Appendix A contains detailed installation instructions.

## MVC and Model2

In the mid-1970s, the MVC (model-view-controller) strategy evolved in the Smalltalk community to reduce coupling between business logic and presentation logic. With MVC, you put your business logic into separate domain objects and isolate your presentation logic in a view, which presents data from domain objects. The controller manages navigation between views, processes user input, and marshals the correct domain objects between the model and view. Good programmers have used MVC ever since, implementing MVC applications using frameworks written in many different languages, including Ruby.

Web developers use a subtly different variant of MVC called *Model2*. Model2 uses the same principles of MVC but tailors them for stateless web applications. In Model2 applications, a browser calls a controller via web standards. The controller interacts with the model to get data and validate user input, and then makes domain objects available to the view for display. Next, the controller invokes the correct view generator, based on validation results or retrieved data. The view layer generates a web page, using data provided by the controller. The framework then returns the web page to the user. In the Rails community, when someone says MVC, they're referring to the Model2 variant.

Model2 has been used in many successful projects spread across many programming languages. In the Java community, Struts is the most common Model2 framework. In Python, the flagship web development framework called Zope uses Model2. You can read more about the model-view-controller strategy at *http://en.wikipedia.org/wiki/Model-view-controller*.

not, go to *http://rubyonrails.org* for more details on Rails installation. Next, here's how to create a Rails project:

```
> rails chapter-1
      create
      create  app/controllers
      create  app/helpers
      create  app/models
      create  app/views/layouts
      create  config/environments
      create  components
      create  db
      create  doc
      create  lib

...

      create  test/mocks/development
      create  test/mocks/test
      create  test/unit
      create  vendor

...
```

```
create  app/controllers/application.rb
create  app/helpers/application_helper.rb
create  test/test_helper.rb
create  config/database.yml
```
...

We truncated the list, but you get the picture.

# Organization

The directories created during installation provide a place for your code, scripts to help you manage and build your application, and many other goodies. Later, we'll examine the most interesting directories in greater detail. For now, let's take a quick pass through the directory tree in the project we created:

*app*

This application organizes your application components. It's got subdirectories that hold the view (*views* and *helpers*), controller (*controllers*), and the backend business logic (*models*).

*components*

This directory holds *components*—tiny self-contained applications that bundle model, view, and controller.

*config*

This directory contains the small amount of configuration code that your application will need, including your database configuration (in *database.yml*), your Rails environment structure (*environment.rb*), and routing of incoming web requests (*routes.rb*). You can also tailor the behavior of the three Rails environments for test, development, and deployment with files found in the *environments* directory.

*db*

Usually, your Rails application will have model objects that access relational database tables. You can manage the relational database with scripts you create and place in this directory.

*doc*

Ruby has a framework, called *RubyDoc*, that can automatically generate documentation for code you create. You can assist *RubyDoc* with comments in your code. This directory holds all the *RubyDoc*-generated Rails and application documentation.

*lib*

You'll put libraries here, unless they explicitly belong elsewhere (such as vendor libraries).

*log*

Error logs go here. Rails creates scripts that help you manage various error logs. You'll find separate logs for the server (*server.log*) and each Rails environment (*development.log*, *test.log*, and *production.log*).

*public*

Like the *public* directory for a web server, this directory has web files that don't change, such as JavaScript files (*public/javascripts*), graphics (*public/images*), stylesheets (*public/stylesheets*), and HTML files (*public*).

*script*

This directory holds scripts to launch and manage the various tools that you'll use with Rails. For example, there are scripts to generate code (*generate*) and launch the web server (*server*). You'll learn much more about using these scripts throughout this book.

*test*

The tests you write and those Rails creates for you all go here. You'll see a subdirectory for mocks (*mocks*), unit tests (*unit*), fixtures (*fixtures*), and functional tests (*functional*). We comprehensively cover testing in Chapter 7.

*tmp*

Rails uses this directory to hold temporary files for intermediate processing.

*vendor*

Libraries provided by third-party vendors (such as security libraries or database utilities beyond the basic Rails distribution) go here.

Except for minor changes between releases, every Rails project will have the same structure, with the same naming conventions. This consistency gives you a tremendous advantage; you can quickly move between Rails projects without relearning the project's organization. The Rails framework itself also relies on this consistency because the different Rails frameworks will often discover files solely on naming conventions and directory structure. For example, later in this example, you'll see the controller invoke views without any custom code.

# The Web Server

Now that we've got a project, let's start a server. Type cd chapter-1 to change to your project directory. Use the *script/server* script to start an instance of the WEBrick server, configured for development. If you're running Windows, preface each call to a script with ruby, and you can use either forward or backward slashes. If you're using a Unix derivative, you can omit the ruby keyword:

```
> ruby script/server
=> Booting WEBrick...
=> Rails application started on http://0.0.0.0:3000
=> Ctrl-C to shutdown server; call with --help for options
[2006-05-11 07:32:08] INFO  WEBrick 1.3.1
```

```
[2006-05-11 07:32:08] INFO  ruby 1.8.4 (2005-12-24) [i386-mswin32]
[2006-05-11 07:32:08] INFO  WEBrick::HTTPServer#start: pid=94884 port=3000
```

Notice a couple of details:

- The server started on port 3000. You can change the port by editing the *script/server* script. See the sidebar "Configuring the Server" for more configuration options.

- We started an instance of WEBrick, a pure Ruby server.

- Ruby will also let you use a backward slash as a path delimiter on the command line, but on Unix you must use the forward slash. Some prefer the backslash because it allows you to use the tab completion feature in the MS-DOS command prompt.

---

### Configuring the Server

If you need to, you can configure the port, the directory for public files, and other server options by modifying the *script/server* script. Here are the default options from that script:

```
...
OPTIONS = {
  :port        => 3000,
  :ip          => "0.0.0.0",
  :environment => "development",
  :server_root => File.expand_path(File.dirname(__FILE__) + "/../public/"),
  :server_type => WEBrick::SimpleServer
}
...
```

You'll often find Ruby configuration written alongside code, especially in scripts like this. The code between { and } is a Ruby hash map. The :key => "value" syntax maps :key to a string "value" in a hash table (OPTIONS in the previous example). Notice the :environment => "development" string; this setting starts the server in the development mode. Among other things, the development mode gives you instant access to any code you change because the web server won't cache code.

---

Point your browser to *http://127.0.0.1:3000/* or *http://localhost:3000/*. You'll see the Rails welcome screen pictured in Figure 1-1. Don't worry about the details of the request yet; for now, know that Rails is running and working correctly.

So far, you've only typed a few words, and you've already set up the build environment and the web server, and verified that the server is running. In the development environment, you'll normally leave the server up, rebooting only to change the database configuration.

*Figure 1-1. The Rails welcome screen*

## Choosing a Server

Rails will run on many different web servers. Most of your development will be done using WEBrick, but you'll probably want to run production code on one of the alternative servers. Let's look briefly at the available servers.

### WEBrick

WEBrick, the default server for Rails, is written entirely in Ruby. It supports the standards you'll need—HTTP for communications, HTML for web pages, and RHTML for embedding Ruby code into web pages for dynamic content. WEBrick has some important advantages:

- It comes with Ruby, so it's free and is always available for your use or for packaging with your projects.
- It's built into Rails, so you don't have to go through any special effort for integration.
- It can make direct calls to your Rails application because they are both written in Ruby.
- It's simple to use.

## Apache

Although WEBrick is the most convenient choice, it's not the most scalable or flexible choice. The Apache web server is the most widely deployed web server in the world. You can choose from an incredible array of plug-ins to run dozens of programming languages or serve other kinds of dynamic content. Apache scales well, with outstanding caching plug-ins and good support for load balancers and *sprayers* (machines that efficiently spread requests across multiple web servers). If you're looking for a safe solution, look no further than the Apache web server.

## lighttpd

Apache is a good general-purpose web server, but it's not the most specialized server. lighttpd is a lightweight web server that's built for one thing: speed. It serves static content such as HTML web pages and images very quickly, and supports applications through an application interface called FastCGI. lighttpd does not have nearly as many flexible plug-ins or the marketing clout of the Apache web server, but if you're looking for a specialized server to serve static content and Rails applications quickly, lighttpd could be your answer. It's fairly young, but it has a great reputation for speed among Rails enthusiasts.

## Mongrel

Although Apache and lighttpd are very fast and scalable production servers, configuring them to serve your Rails application can sometimes be challenging, and it is never as simple as WEBrick. A new web server, Mongrel, may just change all of that. Mongrel combines the advantages of WEBrick (because it's written in Ruby) and lighttpd (because it's written for speed). This combination could make Mongrel an excellent choice for both development and production. It's even younger than lighttpd, but it looks so promising that it has already received backing from a major corporation to speed its development.

## Other web servers

Theoretically, any web server that supports CGI can serve a Rails application. Unfortunately, CGI with Rails is dead slow, so it is really not suitable for production. However, if you are running in a specialized environment that has its own web server, you can probably get it to serve your Rails application using the FastCGI or SCGI interfaces. Do a web search first because it's very likely that someone else has already done it and posted instructions. For example, if you must deploy your Rails application on Microsoft's IIS, you will find that many developers have done this already, and the instructions are easy to find. You'll probably see other web servers rapidly move to support Rails.

Now that your server is up, it's time to write some code. We'll focus on simple controllers and views in the rest of this chapter.

# Creating a Controller

You've seen that Rails organizes applications into pieces with a model, view, and controller. We'll start with the controller. Use the *generate* script (see the sidebar "script/generate") to create a controller. We'll specify the type of object to create first and then the name of the new controller. Type:

```
> ruby script/generate controller Greeting
    exists  app/controllers/
    exists  app/helpers/
    create  app/views/greeting
    exists  test/functional/
    create  app/controllers/greeting_controller.rb
    create  test/functional/greeting_controller_test.rb
    create  app/helpers/greeting_helper.rb
```

You might not have expected to see so much activity. Rails created your expected controller—*greeting_controller.rb*. But you also got a few other files as well:

*application.rb*
> There is not yet a controller for the whole application, so Rails created this one. It will come in handy later as a place to anchor application-wide concerns, such as security.

*views/greeting*
> Rails knows that controllers and views usually come in pairs, so it created a directory called *views/greeting*.

*greeting_controller_test.rb*
> Rails also created a test for your new controller because most Rails developers build automated unit tests to make it easy to build in and maintain quality.

*greeting_helper.rb*
> Rails helpers provide a convenient place to prevent repetition or tedious code from cluttering your views.

Ruby developers created Rails to solve their own problems before generalizing and releasing the tool to solve your problems too. You're seeing an example of excellent experience-based design. Early Rails users noticed that right after creating a controller, they usually needed additional layers of the application, and so they modified the controller generator to save themselves a few keystrokes. *Rails inventors eat their own dog food.*

## Running the Controller

Let's run the application; point your browser to *http://127.0.0.1:3000/greeting*. You'll get an error message telling you that index is an unknown action. Let's find out why. Edit the new controller at the path *app/controller/greeting_controller.rb*:

```
class GreetingController < ApplicationController
end
```

## script/generate

The Rails generator is an impressive productivity booster. It can help you generate all of the basic building blocks for your application. If you forget the options, you can just type ruby script/generate. You'll get the following output:

```
> ruby script/generate
Usage: script/generate [options] generator [args]

General Options:
    -p, --pretend              Run but do not make any changes.
    -f, --force                Overwrite files that already exist.
    -s, --skip                 Skip files that already exist.
    -q, --quiet                Suppress normal output.
    -t, --backtrace            Debugging: show backtrace on erRailss.
    -h, --help                 Show this help
                               message.


Installed Generators
   Builtin: controller, mailer, model, scaffold, web_service
```

Because different generators can create overlapping files, they can be destructive, if you're not careful. Don't worry: Rails gives you quite a bit of help. If you're not sure about the output of a generator, it's best to run it with the --pretend option to see exactly what it might generate.

You can also list the options of any of the installed generators. For example, typing ruby script/generate controller shows you the options for creating a controller.

You can install additional generators. For example, you can use the login generator so that Rails can create the models, views, and controllers for basic authentication architecture. This generator also generates code to handle migration from other versions, scaffolding, and even a web service.

To find the login generator, and other available generators, go to *http://rubyonrails.org/show/Generators*. To install a generator, just use gems. For example, to install the login_generator, type:

```
gem install login_generator -s http://gems.rubyonrails.org
```

You haven't told Rails to do anything yet, so getting some kind of error seems logical. Still, you'll need a little more background before you can fix that problem. Figure 1-2 shows how Rails controllers work.

Rails uses the Action Pack framework to manage controllers. Web browsers communicate with servers by sending requests over the HTTP protocol. For our greeting application, the request was simply to load a URL. The first part of a URL identifies a machine, and the second part identifies a web resource. In the Action Pack, the resource has at least three parts: a controller, some action to perform on a controller,

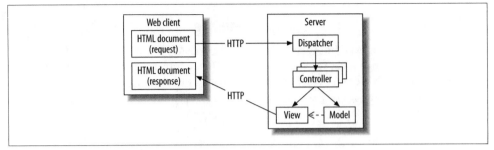

*Figure 1-2. Rails' model-view-controller flow*

and an identifier of a resource. Actions map directly onto controller methods. For example, for this URL:

    http://www.spatulas.com/shopping_cart/total/45

`http://www.spatulas.com/` identifies the web server, `shopping_cart` identifies the controller, `total` identifies the action, and 45 identifies a resource—probably a cart. The web server routes incoming requests to a Ruby script in the Rails framework called the *dispatcher*. Rails has one dispatcher per web server. Next, the Rails dispatcher parses the URL and invokes the appropriate action on the appropriate controller. The controller action may then call the model and ultimately invokes a view.

By default, if you call a controller without specifying an action, Rails calls the `index` action. Now, the error makes more sense. When we specified the URL *app/controller/greeting*, we supplied a controller without an action, so Rails defaulted to a nonexistent index action. You can fix the problem by adding a method called `index` to `GreetingController`. Let's keep things simple by making the `index` method print out HTML directly, as shown in Example 1-1.

*Example 1-1. Rails controller displaying a greeting*

```
class GreetingController < ApplicationController
   def index
      render :text => "<h1>Welcome to your first Rails application<h1>"
   end
end
```

Save your code and reload your browser—you'll get the web page in Figure 1-3. Even though you changed some code, you didn't have to restart the server, redeploy your application, or do anything but reload your browser. This quick turnaround time, called a *rapid feedback loop*, is a hallmark of Ruby and Rails. Often, new Rails developers point to the rapid feedback loop as the feature that affected their productivity more than anything else.

*Figure 1-3. Rendering text from a controller*

# Building a View

You now have a controller that renders text, but this design can take you only so far. If you want to follow Rails MVC conventions, you should render text in a separate view instead of a controller. The sloppy design is easy enough to fix. Instead of printing raw text in a controller, render it in a view. As with many web frameworks, Rails can use a template strategy for the view. For Rails, a template is simply an HTML page with Ruby code mixed in. The Ruby code executes on the server, adding dynamic content to the HTML page.

---

### Documentation

Unlike many open source projects, Rails has excellent documentation. You can find it all at *http://api.rubyonrails.com*. You'll find overviews, tutorials, and even movies. You can always find the API document for the latest version of Ruby on Rails at the site, with a full set of documents for every class in the Rails API. You can also find it with your Rails installation.

The excellent Rails documentation is not an accident. Like Java, Ruby comes with a utility called RubyDoc that generates documentation from source code and comments that you provide within the source code. When you install a gem, it also installs the documentation for the gem. Figure 1-4 shows the documentation for a controller.

---

With Rails, you can generate the view and some helpers that the view will need. Type the generate command to generate a new controller, greeting, with a view, index. (You do this to tie the view and controller together.) When it asks you whether to overwrite the controller, type n for no:

```
> ruby script/generate controller Greeting index
      exists  app/controllers/
```

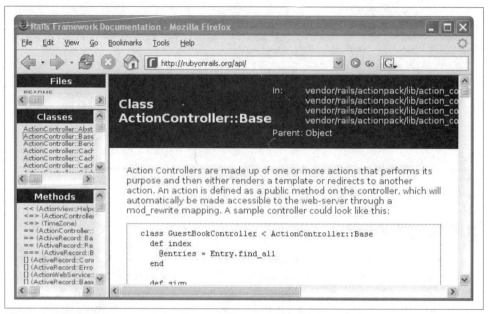

*Figure 1-4. Rails documentation for the controller*

```
      exists  app/helpers/
      exists  app/views/greeting
      exists  test/functional/
   overwrite app/controllers/greeting_controller.rb? [Ynaq] n
        skip  app/controllers/greeting_controller.rb
   overwrite test/functional/greeting_controller_test.rb? [Ynaq] a
   forcing controller
        force  test/functional/greeting_controller_test.rb
        force  app/helpers/greeting_helper.rb
       create  app/views/greeting/index.rhtml
```

The generator created the view, *index.rhtml*, with helper and test files. Keep the index method, so Action Pack can find the action, but take the rest of the code out of the index method:

```
class GreetingController < ApplicationController
   def index
   end
end
```

Unlike most MVC frameworks, you *didn't* specify a view. If your controller doesn't render anything, Rails uses naming conventions to find the right view. The controller's name determines the view's directory, and the controller's method name determines the name of the view. In this case, Action Pack fires the view in *app/view/greeting/index.rhtml*. You didn't have to edit any XML files or type any additional code. You provide consistent naming conventions, and Rails infers your intent.

Now, edit the view. You'll find this data:

```
<h1>Greeting#index</h1>
<p>Find me in app/views/greeting/index.rhtml</p>
```

Reload your browser to see the previous message in HTML. Rails tells you where to find the file, should you ever render an unimplemented view. Rails is full of nice finishing touches like these.

# Tying the Controller to the View

In MVC, the view usually renders model data provided by the controller. Let's set an instance variable in the controller and render it in the view. First, add an instance variable called @welcome_message to the controller:

```
class GreetingController < ApplicationController
  def index
    @welcome_message = "Welcome to your first Rails application"
  end
end
```

Now, display the new message in the view by adding a Ruby expression between <%= and %> tags. Rails renders the value of the expression within these tags, just as if the value of the expression had been printed in place. Here's a view that prints your welcome message as a level one heading:

```
<h1><%= @welcome_message %></h1>
```

Reload. You'll see the same output you got in Example 1-1, though the structure of the application is different. In Example 1-1, you rendered your view within the controller. Here, you built an *RHTML template*. Your HTML tags provided static structure and style, and your Ruby code provided dynamic content; in this case, a variable set within the controller.

## Expressions and Scriptlets

When you're embedding Ruby code, you've got two options. *Scriptlets* are Ruby code, placed between <% and %> tags. Scriptlets rely on side effects, or the *output* of the Ruby code. *Expressions* are Ruby expressions placed between <%= and %> tags. The expression presents the *value* returned by the Ruby code.

You can experiment with the interaction between the controller and view. We've changed the controller and view for greeting to show a few examples of expressions and scriptlets in action. First, we'll set a few values in the controller:

```
class GreetingController < ApplicationController
  def index
    @age=8
    @table={"headings" => ["addend", "addend", "sum"],
```

```
            "body"      => [[1, 1, 2], [1, 2, 3] , [ 1, 3, 4]]
          }
      end
    end
```

Next, here's the view showing expressions and scriptlets, with both interacting with values set in the controller:

```
<h1>Simple expression</h1>
<p>Tommy is <%= @age %> years old.</p>
```

Now, display the value of the instance variable @age, which was set in the controller:

```
<h1>Iteration using scriptlets</h1>
<% for i in 1..5 %>
  <p>Heading number <%= i %> </p>
<% end %>
```

Iterate with a scriptlet and show the current count with an expression:

```
<h1>A simple table</h1>

<table>
  <tr>
    <% @table["headings"].each do |head| %>
      <td>
        <b><%= head %></b>
      </td>
    <% end %>
  </tr>

  <% @table["body"].each do |row| %>
    <tr>
      <% row.each do |col| %>
        <td>
          <%= col %>
        </td>
      <% end %>
    </tr>
  <% end %>

</table>
```

Finally, use both techniques to display the contents of @table.

You'll get the results shown in Figure 1-5.

## Under the Hood

As shown earlier, each time you submit a URL, you're creating an HTTP request, which fires a controller action. Any MVC framework designer needs to decide between reusing the same controller for each request and creating a new controller

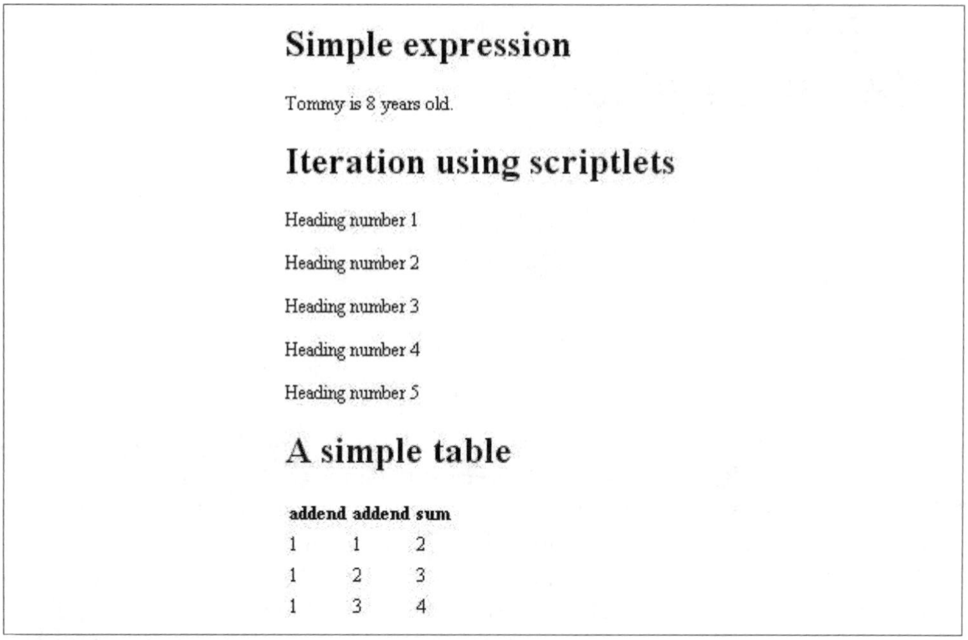

**Simple expression**

Tommy is 8 years old.

**Iteration using scriptlets**

Heading number 1

Heading number 2

Heading number 3

Heading number 4

Heading number 5

**A simple table**

| addend | addend | sum |
|--------|--------|-----|
| 1 | 1 | 2 |
| 1 | 2 | 3 |
| 1 | 3 | 4 |

*Figure 1-5. Results of embedded scriptlets and expressions*

copy per request. Rails does the latter strategy, which it calls *request scope*. Each HTTP request results in a new controller instance, meaning that you'll also get a new set of instance variables for each HTTP request. That's going to affect you in at least two different ways:

- On the plus side, you don't need to worry about threading in your controllers because each request gets a private copy of the controller's instance data.
- On the minus side, it will be harder for you to share instance data between requests. Specifically, if you set instance variables in one controller action method, don't expect to be able to use them in later HTTP requests. You'll need to share them in a session.

# What's Next?

You've created a Rails project. You've created a controller and invoked it from a browser. You've also created a view and learned how views can interact with controllers and with the Ruby language. That's a good foundation, but you've seen only two pieces of the model-view-controller design pattern. In the next chapter, you'll learn how models work. We'll create a database schema and let Rails use the schema to generate our model for us. We'll then use a Rails framework to help manage relationships between the different parts of the application.

# CHAPTER 2
# Active Record Basics

Active Record, which controls the interaction between your application and the database, is the heart of Rails. Active Record's elegant simplicity almost completely eliminates the need for configuration; in this chapter, you'll see how Active Record's conventions reduce your configuration from hundreds of lines to a handful. You'll also see how Active Record's metaprogramming dynamically adds capabilities to your classes, based on the contents and structure of the database. Finally, you'll use Active Record's elegant extensions of Ruby to quickly validate your code with less effort than ever before.

## Active Record Basics

Martin Fowler cataloged the Active Record design pattern in a book called *Patterns of Enterprise Architecture*.* The Rails framework is an implementation of that idea. With any Active Record implementation, users manipulate database tables through record objects. Each record represents a row in a database table, and each Active Record object has CRUD (Create, Read, Update, and Delete) methods for database access. This strategy allows simple designs and straightforward mappings between database tables and application objects.

The Rails persistence framework is like Martin Fowler's Active Record on steroids. The Rails version adds some capabilities that extend Active Record. Table 2-1 shows a list of critical differences, followed by the benefit to the developer.

---

* Design patterns in *Patterns of Enterprise Architecture* appear in an online catalog. The Active Record pattern is defined at *http://www.martinfowler.com/eaaCatalog/activeRecord.html*.

*Table 2-1. Rails versus Active Record*

| Difference | Benefit |
|---|---|
| Rails adds attributes automatically, based on the columns in the database. | Rails developers do not have to specify attributes in more than one place. |
| Rails adds relationship management and validation through a custom internal language. | Rails developers can declare relationships and model-based validation to be managed by the framework without relying on code generation. |
| Rails naming conventions let the database discover specific fields. | Rails developers do not need to configure primary and foreign keys because Active Record discovers them automatically. |

Each Rails enhancement improves readability and reduces the amount of code that you have to write and maintain. You'll find Active Record to be all at once elegant, powerful, and pragmatic.

## Wrapping, Not Mapping

With most Java-based persistence frameworks, you independently build a database table and an object. You then build a map between the two with code or XML configuration. We call this strategy *object relational mapping* (ORM). Java developers usually favor mapping because it can support many different kinds of database schemas. The drawback of ORM is that your code has more repetition because you need to specify each column in the database, in your object model, and often in configuration files, too.

But Active Record uses a wrapping strategy, not a mapping strategy. A Rails developer starts by building a relational database and wraps each table with an Active Record class. Each instance of the class represents a row of the database. The framework then automatically discovers columns from the database table, and dynamically adds them to the Active Record class. Using Active Record, you can build a simple mapping to a typical table in two lines of code.

## A Brief Example

Let's look at a brief Active Record example and walk through the highlights. Then, we'll implement a working Active Record model, and walk through the finer points in more detail. Consider the following Active Record class, which associates many photos to a category:

```
class Photo < ActiveRecord::Base
  belongs_to :category
end
```

This Active Record class is surprisingly complete. There are only a few lines of configuration (versus dozens in a typical Java framework), and no duplication between the model and the schema. Let's break it down:

```
class Photo < ActiveRecord::Base
```

We define a class called Photo that's a subclass of the Base class in the ActiveRecord module. From naming conventions and the name Photo, Active Record knows that this class wraps a database table called photos. That information is enough to let Base query the database system tables for all the columns of photos. Base adds metadata from each column, such as column names, types, and lengths, to Photo. It then adds an attribute to Photo for each column in the database:

```
belongs_to :category
```

Here, you see an example of a *domain-specific language* (DSL). A DSL is created especially to handle a certain domain. This language supports object relational mapping. belongs_to is actually a method of Base, and :category is a Ruby symbol. We use this method to tell Active Record about a many-to-one relationship between Photo (which wraps the table photos) and Category (which wraps the table categories). Through naming conventions, Base discovers the column responsible for managing the relationship. belongs_to then adds the methods and attributes to Photo that users of Book will need to manage the many-to-one relationship. For example, you'll learn later that each Photo object has an attribute called category. So this relationship is nearly trivial to implement, but it adds great power to Rails.

## The Secret Sauce

Each great framework has one or more features that set it apart from the rest. The Rails implementation of Active Record uses a secret sauce composed of three revolutionary ideas:

*Convention over configuration*
> Using Active Record, you'll adhere to a couple of conventions that we'll discuss through the course of the chapter. If you follow the conventions, Active Record can discover most of what it needs to know about the database schema, keeping your code simple and elegant.

*Metaprogramming*
> Active Record discovers features of your database schema and automatically adds them to your object model. For example, Active Record automatically adds to your objects an attribute for every column in your database.

*A language for mapping*
> Active Record uses Ruby to build a language in a language. You'll use a mapping language to specify relationships between your tables.

Each of these ideas is a dramatic departure from what you'd normally see with mapping frameworks. The results, too, are dramatic. You'll find yourself creating more powerful persistent models with less effort than ever before. Let's get to work and see how Active Record works.

# Introducing Photo Share

For the remainder of this book, we'll be working on a single application called Photo Share, a database-backed web application that allows users to share photos among acquaintances. We'll start with these simple requirements, called *user stories*:

- Let a user view a set of photos on the Web so others can see them.
- Organize photos in categories.
- Organize and view slideshows from available photos.

## Defining the Model

Rails is a database-centric development environment, so your development will usually begin with the model. You need to determine the types of objects your application will need. A good starting point is to underline the important nouns in a list of user stories. We've used italic to signify important nouns, so we'll have Active Record classes for photos, categories, and slideshows. We'll also need slides, to keep track of the position of each photo in a slideshow.

There are several important relationships:

- A *category* has many *photos*, and a *photo* can have one or more *categories*.
- A *category* can have other *categories*.
- A *slideshow* has many *slides*.
- A *slide* has one *photo*.

A simple diagram like the one in Figure 2-1 helps to show the entities and relationships in your model. Index cards work well. For many-to-one relationships, we'll use an arrow to mean *belongs to*, so the arrow will point from the one to the many. Two-sided arrows are *many-to-many*, and a line without arrows means *one-to-one*. We'll represent a tree with an arrow that points back to the originating class. We'll use Active Record to define each of these entities and manage each relationship. Now, let's code them in Active Record.

## Configuring Active Record

As always, we start with a Rails project. First, create a Rails project called photos:

```
rails photos
cd photos
```

You've now got a Rails project called photos with three environments: development, test, and production. Rails uses separate databases for each environment (see the

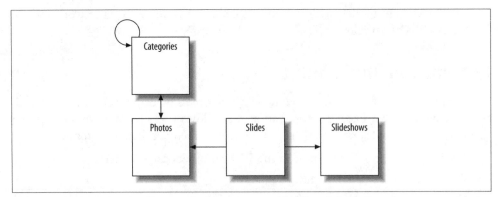

*Figure 2-1. Photos are placed into nested categories and listed in slideshows*

sidebar "Three Databases"). To create a database, make sure the MySQL database is started and also start the *mysql* command prompt:

```
mysql -u <username> -p <password>
```

Now create a database called photos_development:

```
> mysql
...

mysql> create database photos_development;
Query OK, 1 row affected (0.05 sec)
```

Configure your database. This chapter uses a development database, so you need to edit *database.yml* to look like this:

```
development:
  adapter: mysql
  database: photos_development
  username: <your userid>
  password: <your password>
  host: localhost
```

## Schema Migrations

Here, we'll create and configure the development database. We assume that you're working from the MySQL command prompt, but you can easily use another database and any alternative user interface that allows you to update the schema. Keep in mind that it's often useful to be able to execute scripts to create your development database and test data.

 Do not configure your test database as your production or development database. All data in your test database is replaced each time you execute a new test.

You'll need an Active Record model object. Don't worry about the details yet; we'll cover them later. For now, just generate the model object by typing:

```
> ruby script/generate model Photo
    exists  app/models/
    exists  test/unit/
    exists  test/fixtures/
    create  app/models/photo.rb
    create  test/unit/photo_test.rb
    create  test/fixtures/photos.yml
    create  db/migrate
    create  db/migrate/001_create_photos.rb
```

Rails generated a model object in *app/models/photo.rb*, but it won't work without a schema.

So, you have a decision to make. You can manage the schema with SQL scripts or with migrations. If you decide to use simple SQL scripts, you'll need to create database-specific schemas, and you'll probably wind up creating new test data whenever you create a new table. Rails gives a better option: *schema migrations*. You'll have to do a little more work up front, but you'll be able to specify database-independent schemas and improve your database without losing data. The first step is to create a database; then, create a migration for each change you want to make to the database.

To use schema migrations, you'll also need to configure Active Record to use Ruby schemas instead of SQL scripts. If you're running Rails 1.0 or before, edit the *config/ environment.rb* file, and set active.record.schema.format to :ruby, like this:

```
config.active_record.schema_format = :ruby
```

If you're running Rails 1.1 or later, you don't need to do anything because :ruby schemas are the default. Each change you make to the database schema has an up method to make the change, and a down method to undo the change.

Now that we've configured the database, we need a migration. Beginning with Rails 1.1, the model generator creates a migration for you. Look in *db/migrate*, and you'll find a migration called 001_create_photos.rb. You'll also see methods called up and down. Edit them to look like this:

```
class CreatePhotos < ActiveRecord::Migration
  def self.up
    create_table "photos" do |photo|
      photo.column "filename", :string
    end
  end

  def self.down
    drop_table "photos"
  end
end
```

The schema migrations feature keeps track of a list of migrations, and each migration has an associated version number. The up method creates a photos table with two columns, filename and id, and the down method removes it. Each schema migration has steps to do and undo a change. You can include changes that you need to make in data as well. Then, if you need to move back to a previous version, you can do so. But now, we need to run the migration. Type this:

```
> rake migrate
== CreatePhotos: migrating =======================================================
-- create_table("photos")
   -> 0.1250s
== CreatePhotos: migrated (0.1250s) ==============================================
```

You should now verify that Rails created the database schema. Go to the MySQL command prompt, use the photos_development database, and show the tables:

```
> mysql -u root photos_development
Welcome to the MySQL monitor.  Commands end with ; or \g.
Your MySQL connection id is 46 to server version: 5.0.16-nt

Type 'help;' or '\h' for help. Type '\c' to clear the buffer.

mysql> show tables;
+----------------------------+
| Tables_in_photos_development |
+----------------------------+
```

```
| photos          |
| schema_info     |
+-----------------------------+
2 rows in set (0.00 sec)
```

Active Record created two tables: schema_info and photos. In schema_info, Active Record will keep track of the state of the existing version number. You'll be able to keep track of photos using the photos database and keep track of each schema change on that table with a migration. Because migrations handle both data and schema, you'll be able to maintain data across your migrations.

# Basic Active Record Classes

Whether you use migrations or SQL scripts, you'll need to follow the naming conventions. The table name photos and the definition of the id column are both significant. (With our migration, Rails created the id column automatically.) Rails uses several naming conventions:

*Class and table names*
> If the name of your database tables is the English plural of the name of your model class, Rails can usually infer the name of the database table from the name of the Active Record class. (Active Record will have trouble with some irregulars like sheep, but supports many popular irregulars like people.)

*Identifiers*
> Similarly, Active Record automatically finds a column called id and uses it as a unique identifier. The id column should be an integer type, and the column should be populated by the database. In this case, we'll use an auto-increment sequence. Staying with these conventions saves you some configuration, and also makes your code much easier to understand.

*Foreign keys*
> Foreign keys should be named <class>_id. For example, our slides table will have a foreign key named photo_id.

*Capitalization*
> When you're defining a class, capitalize the first letter of each word and omit spaces between words (commonly called *camel casing*). But Rails methods, database table names, columns, attributes, and symbols use underscores to separate words. These conventions are mostly cosmetic, but Rails often uses symbols to refer to a class name, so make sure you follow these conventions. For example, to represent a class called ChunkyBacon, you'd use the symbol :chunky_bacon.

## Wrapping the Table

Now we're ready to look at the Active Record model class we created earlier. In the *app/models* directory (which contains your project's model classes), Rails created the *photo.rb* file, along with some testing code, when we generated our model. Open it:

```
class Photo < ActiveRecord::Base
end
```

Active Record class has all of the information that it needs to wrap the photos table.

## The Rails Console

You'll probably spend a good deal of time in the Rails console, one of the many tools created with each Rails project. The Rails console lets you interactively work with your database-backed models. When you start a console, Rails does the following:

- Connects you to the database
- Loads the Active Record classes in *app/model*
- Lets you interactively work with your model, including database operations

Let's start a console now to manipulate the Photo model we created:

```
ruby script/console
```

We'll use the console to create some new objects, and save them to the database:[*]

```
>> photo=Photo.new
=> #<Photo:0x35301d8 @attributes={"filename"=>""}, @new_record=true>
>> photo.filename = 'cat.jpg'
=> "cat.jpg"
>> photo.save
=> true
```

The new method on Active Record classes can take a code block:

```
>> Photo.new do |dog|
?>    dog.filename = 'dog.jpg'
>>    dog.save
>> end
```

Both techniques create a new model object and save it to the database. Each produces the same SQL, so the choice is entirely a matter of your personal preference.

# Attributes

You've now seen metaprogramming in action through the console. Your applications will use your model objects in the same way. One of the drawbacks of Active

---

[*] After each statement you type, the console will print the value of object.inspect for the last object returned.

Record is the terseness of the source code—it won't tell you much. If you know what's going on under the covers, though, you can easily understand what attributes and methods your class supports.

## Columns

Let's review what happens when Ruby loads the Photo class. From the class name Photo, Active Record infers that the database table name is photos. It then queries the database system tables, which have detailed information about the tables in the database, to get the photos table definition. Next, it places information about the definition of each column into the @@columns class variable. @@columns is an array of Column objects; each column has these attributes:

*name*
> The name of the database column.

*type*

ill generate.

s data is numeric. You'll access it

example, for a database column of

n can be set to null. You'll access it

n can be interpreted as text. You'll

finition.

the Rails unique identifier. You'll
?.

to build dynamic user interfaces.
nique. Normally, you want to get
te's accessors.

## Accessors

You've seen that you can access the database columns of a photo by simply calling an accessor like photo.filename. The Rails implementation isn't necessarily what you'd expect. You might expect to see the accessor for filename as a method on photo. Strangely, if you type:

```
photo.methods.include? 'filename'
```

in the console, you get false, which means that there's no explicit filename accessor for photo. Active Record uses a Ruby metaprogramming trick to attach attributes. It overrides the method_missing method, which gets invoked if you call a nonexistent method of some object. Consider this program:

```
class Talker
  def method_missing(method)
    if method.to_s =~ /say_/
      puts $'
    end
  end
end
```

This Talker class responds to any message beginning with say_, even though no method beginning with say_ exists. For example, Talker.new.say_hello prints hello. Active Record uses this trick to implement accessors. As a consequence, include? returns false for accessors because the class doesn't include an explicit accessor method. You'll see later that Active Record also generates custom finders, like find_by_filename, for each class.

## Identifiers

The id attribute is special to Active Record because that column serves as the primary key for the database table. Our migration created the id column, and a primary key based on the id, automatically. The underlying table definition, shown in Figure 2-2, identifies the primary key with the primary key(id) statement. You might expect Active Record to recognize the unique identifier by seeing which columns are included in a table's primary key, but this strategy is not always possible. Some database managers don't have simple APIs to discover primary or foreign keys, so Active Record uses the id naming convention instead (see Table 2-2).

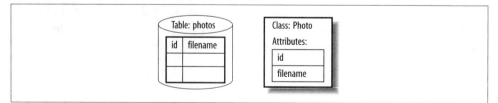

Figure 2-2. The most basic Active Record mapping ties a single table to a model object

## Identifiers and Legacy Schemas

In a typical Rails migration script, you will not see the id column. Rails manages the id field for you by default. In the typical case, Active Record maps the id onto a database sequence, so the database creates the initial value of id. You don't have to let Active Record manage your identifiers. For example, you could have a Photo class with a timestamp attribute called created_at:

```
class Photo < ActiveRecord::Base
  set_primary_key "created_at"
end
```

There are some restrictions, though. The most prominent restriction (as of Rails 1.1) is that you can't use composite keys, or primary keys using more than one database column. If you need to use composite keys, one way to solve the problem is to introduce a new column to serve as your identifier. It need not be the primary key.

Alternatively, you could create a database view. A *view* is a logical view of database data. You can access the results of any query as a view. You could use a view to introduce a new column or to combine several existing columns into one. Active Record could then use the view instead of the table.

Rules for updating views vary across database managers, so depending on your database manager, you'd either have to customize Active Record or use views only for read-only tables. Both approaches have been successfully used in production applications.

*Table 2-2. Active Record adds these methods and attributes to model objects at runtime*

| Features | Purpose |
| --- | --- |
| **Methods** | |
| find_by_<column_name> | Active Record adds a class method to the class for each column in the database, including id. For example, Active Record adds find_by_id, find_by_name and find_by_email to a class wrapping a table having id, name, and email columns. |
| find_by_<column_name>_and_<column_name> | Active Record also adds finders that combine groups of attributes. For example, a Person class wrapping a table with name and email columns would support Person.find_by_name_and_email(name, email). |
| **Attributes** | |
| <column_name> | Active Record creates an attribute with getters and setters for each property in the database. For example, photo.filename = "dog.jpg" would be legal for a photo instance of a class wrapping a table with a filename column. |

# Complex Classes

For Photo Share, we've built an object model in which one table relates to one class. Sometimes, you'll want to map more sophisticated object models to a database table. The two most common scenarios for doing so are inheritance and composition. Let's look at how you'd handle each mapping with Active Record. These examples are not part of our Photo Share application, but the problems are common enough that we will show them to you here.

## Inheritance

Active Record supports inheritance relationships using a strategy called *single-table inheritance*, shown in Figure 2-3. With this kind of inheritance mapping, all descendents of a common class use the same table. For example, a photographer is a person with a camera. With single-table inheritance, all columns for both `Person` and `Photographer` go into the same table. Consider this table:

```
CREATE TABLE people (
    id INT AUTO_INCREMENT NOT NULL,
    type VARCHAR(20),
    name VARCHAR(20),
    email VARCHAR(30),
    camera VARCHAR(20),
    PRIMARY KEY (id)
);
```

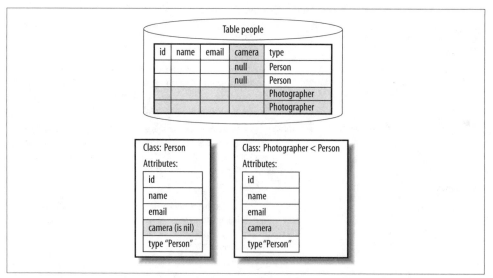

*Figure 2-3. Rails supports single-table inheritance between an entity (Person) and subclass (Photographer)*

A query against Person will return people and photographers. Active Record doesn't need to build any special support to handle a query against a superclass. Subclasses are more difficult. In order to allow a query returning only Photographers, Active Record must have some way to determine the type of an object for an individual row. Active Record uses the type field for this purpose.

Now, we need classes, which are trivial:

```
class Photographer < Person
end

class Person < ActiveRecord::Base
end
```

We declare Photographer as a subclass of Person. Active Record will manage the type attribute and everything else. You'll be able to access the camera property from Photographer. We don't need these classes for Photo Share, so we'll delete them.

You've probably noticed that Active Record's implementation of inheritance is not true inheritance because all items in an inheritance tree have the same attributes. In our example, all people have cameras even if they are not photographers. In practice, that limitation is not severe. A parent can ignore attributes introduced by subclasses. This strategy is a compromise. You get slightly better performance (because fewer tables means fewer joins) and simplicity at the cost of muddying the abstraction a little.

 Normally, only Active Record needs to set the type attribute. Be careful when you need to manage type yourself. You can't say person.type because type is a class method on Object. If you need to see the value of the type field, use person[:type] instead.

## Composition

If you want to extend a Person class with Address, you can use a has_one relationship, or you can use composition. Composition works well when you want to use a pervasive type like address or currency across many Active Record models. You'll use composed_of for this type of relationship, as shown in Figure 2-4.

Let's look at a Person that is composed_of an Address. In a composition relationship, there's a main class (Person) and one or more component classes (Address). Each component class explicitly references one or more database columns. Start with a table that's defined like this:

```
CREATE TABLE people (
    id INT AUTO_INCREMENT NOT NULL,
    type VARCHAR(20),
    name VARCHAR(20),
    email VARCHAR(30),
    street_address VARCHAR(30),
```

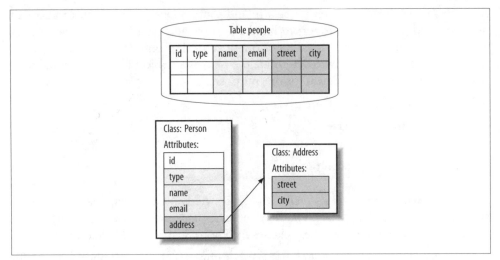

*Figure 2-4. Composed of maps many objects onto one table*

```
    city VARCHAR(30),
    state VARCHAR(20),
    zip INTEGER(5),
    camera VARCHAR(20),
    PRIMARY KEY (id)
);
```

You then map the table onto two different classes. First, create a Person class with a composed_of relationship:

```
class Person < ActiveRecord::Base
  composed_of :address, :class_name => "Address",
              :mapping => [[:street_address, :street_address],
                           [:city, :city],
                           [:state, :State],
                           [:zip, :zip]]
end
```

If the first parameter for composed_of and the name of the component class are the same, Active Record can infer the name of the component class. Otherwise, you can override it with a :class_name modifier. For example, you can use composed_of person_address class_name => "Address". Next, create an Address class:

```
class Address
  def initialize(street_address, city, state, zip)
    @street_address = street_address
    @city = city
    @state = state
    @zip = zip
  end

  attr_reader :street_address, :city, :state, :zip
end
```

Address is the component class. For each database column that the component represents, the component class must have an attribute and a parameter in the `initialize` method:

```
>> elvis=Person.new
>> elvis.name="Elvis Presley"
>> elvis.email= "elvis@graceland.com"
>> address=Address.new("3734 Elvis Presley Blvd", "Memphis", "Tennessee", 38118)
>> elvis.address=address
>> elvis.save
>> puts elvis.address.street_address
3734 Elvis Presley Blvd
```

Though `street_address`, `city`, `state`, and `zip` are columns on the people table, you don't use those attributes on any `Person` object directly. Instead, access these attributes through the `address` attribute on `Person`. Table 2-3 shows the attributes added by a `composed_of` relationship.

*Table 2-3. Metaprogramming for composed_of :class*

| Attributes | Description |
| --- | --- |
| `<class>` | The component class (`person.address`) |
| `<class>_<attribute>` | Attributes for the component class (`person.address_zip`) |

# Behavior

Active Record lets you manipulate and find table data directly through Active Record classes and instances. If you want to work with data from a table, use the class. If you want to work with a table row, use an instance. `ActiveRecord::Base` class supplies many of the methods, and `missing_method` provides most of the rest. You can find the documentation for the latest stable Active Record version online at the following address: *http://api.rubyonrails.com*.

## Finders

You can use other finders as well. `find_by_sql` lets you type SQL directly into a finder; `find_all` returns all records. In addition, Active Record adds a custom finder called `find_by_<column_name>` to each model class for each column in that model's table.

Let's use some of the methods on `Photo`. We'll use a finder and the `destroy` method to delete an object from the database:

```
Photo.find_by_filename("balboa_park.jpg").destroy
```

The methods delete and destroy are slightly different. delete aborts on minor errors, but destroy does not abort unless there's a critical database error. You can also update objects. Let's update the Photo object for *cat.jpg*:

```
>> cat=Photo.find_by_filename "cat.jpg"
...
>> cat.filename="Cat.jpg"
...
>> cat.update
...
>> puts cat.reload.filename
Cat.jpg
...
```

In this case, we found the *cat.jpg* record. We next updated the filename attribute and called update to write the changes to the database.

## Validation

So far, you've used Active Record to do database operations on an object. You can also use Active Record for simple validation. For example, you can verify that the filename property exists with one line of code. Change the Photo class in *app/models/photo.rb* to look like this:

```
class Photo < ActiveRecord::Base
  validates_presence_of :filename
end
```

Let's see how the validation works. Go back to the console (you'll need to restart it to reload your changes), and try to save a blank photo:

```
>> photo=Photo.new
=> #<Photo:0x3501b70 @attributes={"filename"=>""}, @new_record=true>
>> photo.save
=> false
```

The save failed. Let's find out why:

```
>> photo.errors.each {|attribute, error| puts attribute + ": " +error}
filename: can't be blank
=> {"filename"=>["can't be blank"]}
```

You can do several different kinds of validation, or you can create your own. You could validate an email message like this:

```
validates_format_of :email,
                    :with => /^([^@\s]+)@((?:[-a-z0-9]+\.)+[a-z]{2,})$/i
```

Or you could validate the length of a field like this:

```
validates_length_of :name, :within => 6..100
```

Later, you'll see that the Rails view integration uses this information to present meaningful error messages; look for those details in Chapter 5. You've seen the basics of working with Active Record classes. You use a model object or its class to directly manipulate rows in the database table. Active Record goes beyond most traditional wrapping frameworks because it helps you manage relationships between tables. In the next few sections, let's look into how Active Record manages simple relationships.

## Transactions

Photo Share doesn't require transactions, but for many applications, transactional behavior is critical. If you have some code that must be executed as a single unit, you can use Active Record transactions. The most common example is a transfer between two accounts. A transfer is fundamentally a debit and a credit. The Ruby code for a transfer between from and to Active Record Account models might look like this:

```
def transfer(from, to, amount)
  from.debit(amount)
  to.credit(amount)
end
```

You wouldn't want this method to fail after the debit—if it did, the holder of the from account would be shorted by amount. So you use a transaction. This is the way it works:

```
def transfer(from, to, amount)
  Account.transaction do
    from.debit(amount)
    to.credit(amount)
  end
end
```

transaction is a method on all Active Record classes. With this approach, you can maintain the integrity of your transactions.

# Moving Forward

In the next chapter, we'll look at managing relationships between Active Record classes. We'll see most types of Active Record relationships in action, including:

- belongs_to
- has_one
- has_many
- has_and_belongs_to_many
- acts_as_list
- acts_as_tree

We'll build each of these into our evolving Photo Share object model. Then, we'll take a very quick look at two other relationships: inheritance and composition. By the end of the next chapter, we'll have a fully functioning, database-backed object model.

# CHAPTER 3
# Active Record Relationships

Dealing with relationships is one of the most important jobs of persistence frameworks. The best persistence frameworks handle relationships with excellent performance for the end user and simplicity for the developer. Active Record takes advantage of the Ruby language and naming conventions to simplify both access and configuration of related data. In this chapter, we'll focus on building relationships between tables, and reflecting those relationships in your model objects.

With validation, shown in the previous chapter, you began to see the domain-specific language built into Active Record. We'll use that language to define relationships between the objects in our database. Three components specify a relationship: the relationship itself, the association or target, and named parameters. More precisely, these are:

*relationship*
> A method, defined through `ActiveRecord::Base`, which defines the behavior of the relationship.

*association(s)*
> A symbol that specifies the target of the relationship. The symbol may be singular or plural, based on the cardinality of the target.

*named parameters*
> Like all Ruby methods, the relationship can take an optional number of named parameters, which may also have default values.

A statement defining a relationship has the form:

```
relationship :association :parameter1 => value, :parameter2 => value, ...
```

For example, you might have:

```
class Slideshow < ActiveRecord::Base
  has_many :photos :order => position
```

Using this small amount of language, you'll be able to define complex relationships quickly. Your relationships will also be easy to read and maintain. Let's implement the full model for Photo Share, complete with relationships.

---

### Relational Database Relationships

Relational databases are fundamentally based on different kinds of relationships between tables. A set of table columns called *keys* provides the structure for all relationships. A *primary key* is a set of columns in a table that uniquely identify a row within that same table. A *foreign key* is a set of columns in a table that uniquely identifies a row in another table. A database manager can *join* two tables by matching the primary keys in one table to the foreign keys in another. Active Record also uses primary and foreign keys to manage relationships. Unlike relational databases, Active Record limits its identifiers to a single database column.

---

# belongs_to

The most common database relationship is many-to-one. Figure 3-1 shows how Active Record maps the "many" side of such a relationship. In Photo Share, we want users to be able to build slideshows. A slideshow contains an ordered list of pictures. We can't simply use pictures in a slideshow because a picture has no way of keeping its position in a slideshow, so we'll introduce a Slide class. We'll then need a many-to-one relationship between slides and slideshows: a slideshow consists of many slides, but each slide (a photo combined with a position) can belong to only one slideshow. To give us the flexibility that we need (we'll also want the ability to reuse photos in different slideshows), we'll need another relationship between photos and slides, but let's leave that for later.

As before, let's create our database tables in a migration, so it will be easy to back out any unnecessary changes. Generate a model and migration to create a new class for Slide, and another for Slideshow:

```
ruby script/generate model Slideshow
ruby script/generate model Slide
```

Rails generates the models and migrations for slideshows and slides. Now, edit the new migration in *db/migrate/create_slideshow.rb*. As before, we'll create steps to migrate up and down. The up step will create the slides and slideshows tables, and the down step will drop them, like this:

```
class CreateSlideshows < ActiveRecord::Migration
  def self.up
    create_table "slideshows" do |t|
      t.column "name", :string
      t.column "created_at", :datetime
```

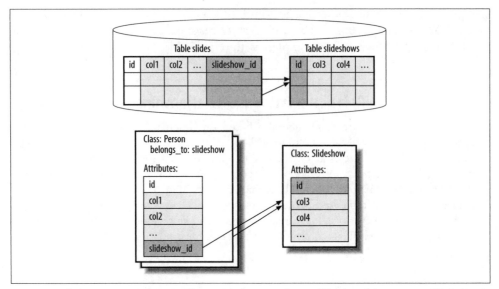

*Figure 3-1. belongs_to :association relationship between Entity (Slide) and Association (Slideshow)*

```
    end
  end

  def self.down
    drop_table "slideshows"
  end
end
```

Edit the new migration in *db/migrate/create_slide.rb*, like this:

```
class CreateSlides < ActiveRecord::Migration
  def self.up
    create_table "slides" do |t|
      t.column "position", :integer
      t.column "photo_id", :integer
      t.column "slideshow_id", :integer
    end
  end

  def self.down
    drop_table "slides"
  end
end
```

You can now run the migrations:

```
rake migrate
```

If you want, you can verify that you have slide and slideshow tables in your database. If you decide that adding these tables was a huge mistake, you could back up to the previous version by typing rake migrate VERSION=1, which would run the down method in all migrations greater than 1, starting with the greatest. You can move to any version number in this way. Be careful, though: if your migration drops a table, you'll lose that data.

At this point, some data to test the new relationships would be nice. Because we're not running these in formal tests or in production, let's create some simple SQL scripts.* Create a script called *slideshow_data.sql*:

```
insert into slideshows values (1, 'Interesting pictures', now());
insert into slides values (1,  1, 1, 1);
insert into slides values (2,  2, 2, 1);
insert into slides values (3,  3, 3, 1);
insert into slides values (4,  4, 4, 1);
insert into slides values (5,  5, 5, 1);
insert into slides values (6,  6, 6, 1);
insert into slides values (7,  7, 7, 1);
insert into slides values (8,  8, 8, 1);
insert into slides values (9,  9, 9, 1);
insert into photos values (1,  "balboa_park.jpg");
insert into photos values (2,  "camel.jpg");
insert into photos values (3,  "cat_and_candles.jpg");
insert into photos values (4,  "hut.jpg");
insert into photos values (5,  "mosaic.jpg");
insert into photos values (6,  "polar_bear.jpg");
insert into photos values (7,  "police.jpg");
insert into photos values (8,  "sleeping_dog.jpg");
insert into photos values (9,  "stairs.jpg");
```

First, migrate down to zero and back up by typing rake migrate VERSION=0 and then rake migrate to make sure that you're starting from scratch. These commands will drop all of the tables and create them again. Start the MySQL prompt, type use photos_development, and execute the script by typing source db/slideshow_data.sql at the MySQL prompt. Now that you have working tables, you can edit the new model in *app/models/slide.rb*. Add the relationship between slides and slideshows to the new Slide model class:

```
class Slide < ActiveRecord::Base
  belongs_to :slideshow
  belongs_to :photo
end
```

Save your changes, and you've got a working belongs_to relationship from Slide to Slideshow and another from Slide to Photo. To see it in action, go back to the Rails console. (If you closed the console, type ruby script/console to restart it.) Type the lines in bold:

```
>> slide = Slide.find 1
=> ...
>> slide.photo.filename
```

---

* You normally wouldn't need to create test data in this way. You would use text fixtures, and load the fixtures with the command rake load fixtures. See Chapter 7 for more details on using test fixtures.

```
=> "balboa_park.jpg"
>> slide.slideshow.name
=> "Interesting pictures"
```

belongs_to introduces the photo and slideshow instance variables on slide, and also some behavior. Table 3-1 shows the methods added to the model by the belongs_to method.

*Table 3-1. Metaprogramming for belongs_to and has_one*

| Added Feature | Description |
|---|---|
| **Methods** | |
| <association>.nil? | Test the association for a nil value: |
| | `slide.photo.nil?` |
| build_<association> | Build an object of the associated type. Do not initialize the built object to the root object: |
| | `slide.build_photo(:filename => "cat.jpg"` |
| | In this example, photo.slide is initialized to nil. |
| create_<association> | Create an object of the associated type, initialized to the root object. It takes a hash map of attributes for the new object as a parameter: |
| | `slide.create_photo({:filename => "cat.jpg", :name => "cat"}` |
| **Attributes** | |
| <association> | An attribute of the type of the associated object: |
| | `belongs_to :photo on Slide allows slide.photo and slide.photo = nil` |

belongs_to is only the "many" end of a many-to-one relationship. Let's look at the "one" side.

# has_many

We'll need to implement has_many relationships on both Photo and Slideshow. Figure 3-2 shows the mapping between Active Record objects and database tables with has_many.

has_many is the other side of a belongs_to relationship, so you don't need to modify the class or table for Slide. You can merely add the relationship has_many to *slideshow.rb*:

```
class Slideshow < ActiveRecord::Base
  has_many :slides
end
```

And now, *photo.rb*:

```
class Photo < ActiveRecord::Base
  has_many :slides
  validates_presence_of :filename
end
```

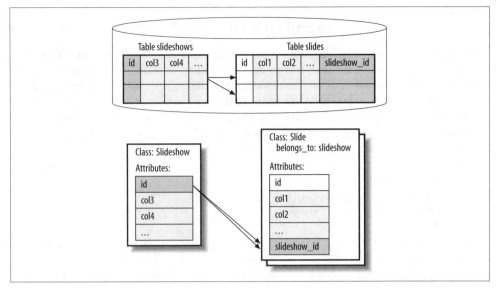

*Figure 3-2. The entity (slideshow) has_many associations (slides) relationship is a one-to-many relationship*

By specifying that a photo has many slides, you give users the ability to use the same photo in several different slideshows. Remember: a slide is a photo and a position in a specific slideshow. So a slide can't be reused, but a photo can.

That's all you have to do to manage the second side of the relationship. Now, you can to see all of the slides associated with a photo, and all of the slides in a slideshow. As usual, you can open the console to see the model in action:

```
>> slide = Slide.find 1
...
>> slideshow = slide.slideshow
...
>> slideshow.slides.each {|slide| puts slide.photo.filename}
balboa_park.jpg
camel.jpg
cat_and_candles.jpg
hut.jpg
mosaic.jpg
polar_bear.jpg
police.jpg
sleeping_dog.jpg
stairs.jpg
```

So you get a list of slides in the slideshow, and each has an associated photo. Active Record is now managing the has_many relationship between Slideshow and Slide. You could use photo.slides in the same way. Table 3-2 shows you the metaprogramming for has_many.

# Cascading Relationships

Many-to-one relationships introduce some problems for persistence frameworks. Primarily, the framework designer has to decide whether deleting a parent object also deletes child objects as well. Automatic deletion of dependent objects is called *cascading deletes*. Sometimes, you want automatic deletion to happen. For example, deleting an invoice should also delete the line items for that invoice. But sometimes, you want related objects to stay: employees should not be deleted when a department is dissolved. If you define a relationship with the :dependent option, deleting a row also deletes the associated objects. For example, to define an invoice, you might specify your invoice like this:

```
class Invoice < ActiveRecord::Base
  has_many :line_items, dependent => true
end
```

With this definition, deleting an invoice would also delete associated line items, each with a separate query. Sometimes, using a separate query to delete each child is unnecessarily inefficient, but there's a remedy. If the line items belong to one invoice—and only one—you can set the exclusively_dependent parameter on has_many to true, and Active Record will delete all dependent objects with one query.

Similarly, when you *read* an object, you need to decide whether to load dependent objects. By default, Active Record does not cascade loads. But you can load children when you load a parent by using the :include option on any finder.

*Table 3-2. Metaprogramming for has_many*

| Added feature | Description |
|---|---|
| **Methods** | |
| `<associations><< object` | Add an object to the `<associations>` collection:<br>`photo.slides << a_slide` |
| `<associations>.delete object` | Delete an object in the `<associations>` collection. The objects will be destroyed if the dependent parameter of `has_many` is set to `true`:<br>`photo.slides.delete a_slide` |
| `<associations>_singular_ids collection` | Replace the `<associations>` collection with a collection of objects identified by `ids` in the collection:<br>`photo.slides_singular_ids [1, 2, 3, 4]` |
| `<associations>.find` | Uses the same rules as a basic find, but operates only on the items in the `<associations>` collection:<br>`photo.slides.find_by_position 4` |
| `<associations>.clear` | Delete all of the objects in the association:<br>`photo.slides.clear` |
| `<associations>.empty?` | Test to see if `<associations>` collection is empty:<br>`photo.slides.clear` |

*Table 3-2. Metaprogramming for has_many (continued)*

| Added feature | Description |
|---|---|
| `<associations>.size` | Return the number of items in the `<associations>` collection:<br>`photo.slides.size` |
| `<associations>.build` | Build an object of the associated type, but do not initialize it to the root object. It takes a hash map of attributes for the new object as a parameter:<br>`slide.build_photo(:filename => "cat.jpg"`<br>In this example, `photo.slide` is initialized to `nil`. |
| `<associations>.create` | Create an object of the associated type, initialized to the root object. It takes a hash map of attributes for the new object as a parameter:<br>`slide.build_photo(:filename => "cat.jpg"`<br>In this example, `photo.slide` is initialized to `slide`. |
| **Attributes** | |
| `<associations>` | A collection of the associated objects:<br>`slide.photos[4]` |

# has_one

The simplest database relationship is the one-to-one relationship. With Active Record, you can implement one-to-one relationships with either belongs_to or has_one. You decide whether to use belongs_to or has_one based on where the foreign key resides. The class associated to the table with the primary key uses belongs_to, and the other uses has_one. Figure 3-3 shows a has_one relationship.

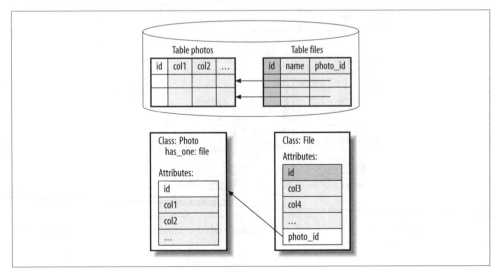

*Figure 3-3. In this one-to-one relationship, a Photo has_one File*

Let's take a simple example. Hypothetically, you could have decided to implement photos and files in separate tables. If you put a foreign key called photo_id into the files table, you would have this Active Record Photo class:

```
class Photo < ActiveRecord::Base
  has_one :file
  ...
end
```

has_one is identical to belongs_to with respect to metaprogramming. For example, adding either has_one :photo or belongs_to :photo to Slide would add the photo attribute to Slide. We really have no need for adding an extra table to manage a file, so let's move on to the next relationship.

## has_and_belongs_to_many

Many-to-many relationships are more complex than the three relationships shown so far, because these relationships require an additional table in the database. Rather than relying on a single foreign key column, you'll need a *relationship table*. Each row of a relationship table expresses a relationship with foreign keys, but has no other data. Figure 3-4 shows our relationship table.

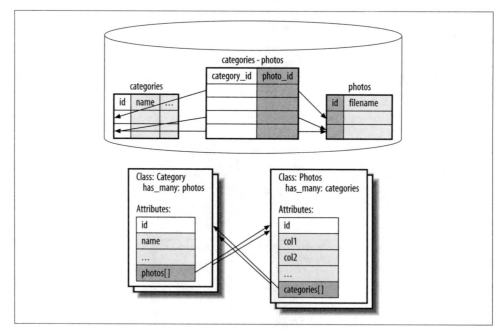

*Figure 3-4. A has_and_belongs_to_many association builds a many-to-many relationship through a join table*

Photo Share requires a many-to-many relationship between `Photo` and `Category`. A category can hold many photos, and the same photo can fit into more than one category. As always, you'll start with the database. You'll need to create a table called categories to hold all categories. You'll also need a relationship table. The Active Record naming convention for the relationship table is `classes1_classes2`, with the classes in alphabetical order, so you need to generate a migration for the categories table:

```
ruby script/generate model Category
```

This generation step creates a migration containing the model table but not the relationship table. This migration will be a little different. Each photo should be in a category. For our migration, create a default category called `All`, and place each photo into that category. Edit your migration, and make it look like this:

```
class CreateCategories < ActiveRecord::Migration
  def self.up
    create_table "categories" do |t|
      t.column "name", :string
      t.column "parent_id", :integer
    end
    create_table("categories_photos", :id=>false) do |t|
      t.column "category_id", :integer
      t.column "photo_id", :integer
    end
    Category.new do |category|
      category.name = "All"
      Photo.find(:all).each do |photo|
        photo.categories << category
        photo.save
      end
    end
  end

  def self.down
    drop_table "categories"
    drop_table "categories_photos"
  end
end
```

That code is simple enough. The new migration creates two tables: one for categories and one as a join table to manage relationships between our categories and photos. categories is not a model table, so it needs no id. Because we don't want an id column on our join table, we used the parameter `:id => false` when we created categories_photos. But we're not ready to run the migration until we've created our model objects and defined the relationships between photos and categories. You can't run the migration yet, though. There's no model class for photos, and no relationship between `Photo` and `Category`.

Category needs a many-to-many relationship, with the exceedingly verbose Ruby method has_and_belongs_to_many :photos:

```
class Category < ActiveRecord::Base
  has_and_belongs_to_many :photos
end
```

You'll also need to add a many-to-many relationship to the Photo class:

```
class Photo < ActiveRecord::Base
  validates_presence_of :filename

  has_many :slides
  has_and_belongs_to_many :categories
end
```

This code adds the categories collection to Photo, and the photos collection to Category. Now, you can run the migration. Type:

```
rake migrate
```

You can verify that it worked in the console. From the console, type:

```
all = Category.find :first
all.photos.each {|photo| puts photo.filename}
```

You still get a full view of what's going on with categories. Once again, you need some data to illustrate what's going on. Add the following to the end of *photos_data.sql*:

```
insert into categories values (1, 'All', null);
insert into categories values (2, 'People', 1);
insert into categories values (3, 'Animals', 1);
insert into categories values (4, 'Places', 1);
insert into categories values (5, 'Things', 1);
insert into categories values (6, 'Friends', 2);
insert into categories values (7, 'Family', 2);
insert into categories_photos values (4, 1);
insert into categories_photos values (3, 2);
insert into categories_photos values (3, 3);
insert into categories_photos values (4, 4);
insert into categories_photos values (5, 5);
insert into categories_photos values (3, 6);
insert into categories_photos values (2, 7);
insert into categories_photos values (4, 8);
insert into categories_photos values (4, 9);
insert into categories_photos values (4, 7);
```

Now, you can see how categories are working inside the console:

```
>> category = Category.find_by_name "Animals"
...
>> category.photos.each {|photo| puts photo.filename}
camel.jpg
cat_and_candles.jpg
polar_bear.jpg
>> photo.filename = "cat.jpg"
=> "cat.jpg"
```

As expected, you get an array called photos on category that's filled with photos that are associated in the join table categories_photos. Let's add a photo:

```
>> photo.filename = "cat.jpg"
...
>> photo.save
=> true
>> category.photos << photo
...
>> category.save
```

Look a little closer at this statement: category.photos << photo. (It adds a photo to category.photos.) But the save is changing neither the photos nor the categories table. It's actually adding a row to the categories_photos table. This type of relationship is the only instance in which an Active Record class does not map directly to the rows and columns of a database table. The methods and attributes added by the has_ and_belongs_to_many method are identical to those added by has_many and are shown in Table 3-2.

### Join models

You might wonder whether it's possible to create a Rails model from the categories_ photos table. As of Rails 1.0, you couldn't do such a thing. Now, with new join models in Rails 1.1, it's easy. You can use has_many and belongs_to with the through parameter. For example, you could easily decide to map slides in this way:

```
class Slideshow < ActiveRecord::Base
  has_many :photos :through => :slides
end
```

This example creates database tables, through migrations or other means, for photos, slideshows, and slides. The relationship table also serves as a relationship table, and a first class model. The structure in the example is slightly different from a typical join table. The primary differences are these:

- The Slide is a first class model.
- You can add attributes to Slide.
- You can use :through with has_many, belongs_to, and has_and_belongs_to_many.

The :through relationship makes it possible to build much more sophisticated relationships, allowing you to identify and tag each relationship with additional data, as required.

# acts_as_list

Active Record has three special relationships that let you explicitly model lists, trees, and nested sets: acts_as_list, acts_as_tree, and acts_as_nested_set, respectively. We'll look at the two relationships required by Photo Share in this chapter: acts_as_ list and acts_as_tree. acts_as_list lets you express items as an ordered list and also provides methods to move items around in the hierarchy. Figure 3-5 shows the mapping. In Photo Share, we'll use `acts_as_list` to model a slideshow, which is an ordered list of slides. Later, we'll use `acts_as_tree` to manage our nested categories.

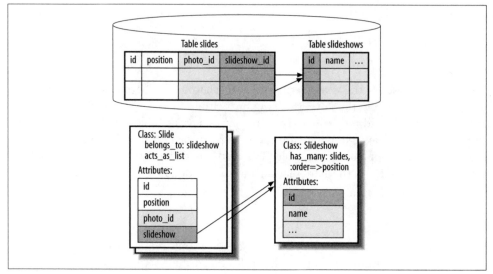

*Figure 3-5. acts_as_list allows an explicit ordering*

First, let's create the slideshow. We want users to be able to move slides up and down in a show. We'll use the existing slides and add the Active Record relationship `acts_as_list`:

```
class Slide < ActiveRecord::Base
  belongs_to :slideshow
  acts_as_list :scope => "slideshow_id"
  belongs_to :photo
end
```

This example builds a list of slides that comprise a slideshow. `belongs_to` is a one-to-many relationship, imposing structure. `acts_as_list` is a helper relationship, imposing order and introducing behavior. To Active Record, each relationship is independent. The `Slide` model has a `belongs_to` relationship with both `Slideshow` and `Photo` parents. You use the `:scope` parameter to tell Active Record which items belong in the list. In this case, we want the list to contain all slides related to a slideshow, so set the `:scope` parameter to `:slideshow_id`.

To capture ordering, Active Record uses a `position` attribute by default. Because you have a position column in the database, you don't need to do anything more to the slides to support the list. However, you'll want the array of slides to be fetched and displayed in the right order, so make one small change to `Slideshow`:

```
class Slideshow < ActiveRecord::Base
  has_many :slides, :order => :position
end
```

We're ready to use the list. You can use methods added by `acts_as_list` to change the order of slides in the slideshow, and to indicate which items are first and last:

```
>> show = Slideshow.find 1
...
>> show.slides.each {|slide| puts slide.photo.filename}
cat_and_candles.jpg
hut.jpg
mosaic.jpg
polar_bear.jpg
police.jpg
sleeping_dog.jpg
stairs.jpg
balboa_park.jpg
camel.jpg
>> show = Slideshow.find 1
=> #<Slideshow:0x3901778 @attributes={"name"=>"Interesting pictures", "id"=>"1",
 "created_at"=>"2006-05-11 14:57:06"}>
>> show.slides.first.photo.filename
=> "cat_and_candles.jpg"
>> show.slides.first.move_to_bottom
=> true
>> show.slides.last.photo.filename
=> "camel.jpg"
>> show.reload
=> #<Slideshow:0x3901778 @slides=nil, @attributes={"name"=>"Interesting pictures
", "id"=>"1", "created_at"=>"2006-05-11 14:57:06"}>
>> show.slides.last.photo.filename
=> "cat_and_candles.jpg"
>>
```

By convention, positions start at 1 and are sequentially numbered through the end of the list. Position 1 is the top, and the biggest number is the bottom. You can move any item higher or lower, move items to the top or bottom, create items in any position, and get relative items in the list, as in Table 3-3. Keep in mind that moving something higher means making the position smaller, so you should think of the position as a priority. Higher positions mean higher priorities, so they'll be closer to the front of the list.

Table 3-3 shows all the methods added by the `acts_as_list` relationship. Keep in mind that you'll use `acts_as_list` on objects that already have a `belongs_to` relationship, so you'll also get the methods and attributes provided by `belongs_to`. You'll also inherit the methods from array, so `slideshow.slides[1]` and `slideshow.slides.first` are both legal.

*Table 3-3. Metaprogramming features for acts_as_list*

| Added feature—methods | Description |
| --- | --- |
| `increment_position` | Increments the position attribute of this list element:<br>`slideshow.slides[1].increment_position` |
| `decrement_position` | Decrement the position attribute of this list element:<br>`slideshow.slides[2].decrement_position` |
| `higher_item` | Return the previous item in the list. Higher means closer to the front, or closer to index 1, as in priority:<br>`slideshow.slides[2].higher_item` |
| `lower_item` | Return the next item in the list. Lower means closer to the back, or farther from index 1, as in priority:<br>`slideshow.slides[1].lower_item` |
| `in_list?` | Test whether an object has been added to a list:<br>`slide.in_list?` |
| `insert_at position` | Insert the current item at a given position. Default is position 1:<br>`slide.insert_at(1)` |
| `first?` | Return `true` if `position==1`; `false` otherwise:<br>`slide.first?` |
| `last?` | Return `true` if position is the largest in the list; return `false` otherwise:<br>`slideshow.slides[7].last?` |
| `move_higher` | Move this item toward index 1:<br>`slideshow.slides[4].move_lower` |
| `move_lower` | Move this item away from index 1:<br>`slideshow.slides[3].move_higher` |
| `move_to_top` | Move this item to index 1:<br>`slideshow.slides[3].move_to_top` |
| `move_to_bottom` | Make this item the last in the list:<br>`slideshow.slides[3].move_to_bottom` |
| `remove_from_list` | Remove this item from the list:<br>`slideshow.slides[3].remove_from_list` |

# Trees

Let's think about the most complex relationship: nested categories. you could implement categories by adding `belongs_to :category` and `has_many :categories` to the Category class. The code would not be easy to read because a category would have an instance variable called category (for the parent) and another instance variable called categories for the children. What would be better are instance variables called parent and children, but you'd be forced to override Active Record naming conventions and to write much more code.

This arrangement is common enough that Active Record has the `acts_as_tree` relationship, shown in Figure 3-6. As you would expect, `acts_as_tree` requires a foreign key called parent_id by default. If you use the name parent_id, Active Record discovers and uses that foreign key to organize the tree structure. As always, if you need to override this name, you can do so. Each node of the tree points to its parent, and the root of the tree is null.

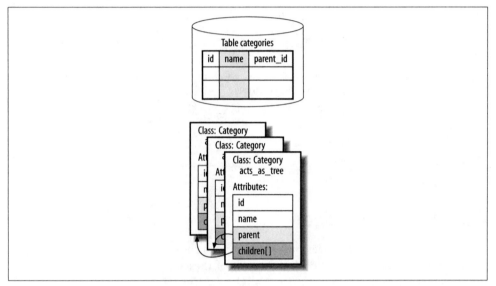

*Figure 3-6. The acts_as_tree relationship is recursive, with an entity (Category) acting as both parent and children*

You've already got a Category class and a database table behind it with a parent_id. Let's let Active Record manage the category tree:

```
class Category < ActiveRecord::Base
  has_and_belongs_to_many :photos
  acts_as_tree
end
```

If you'd like, you can order the children with :order modifier as we did in the favorites example, but you don't have to. The tree is ready to use as is. You can already work with the tree from within the console:

```
>> root = Category.find_by_name 'All'
...
>> puts root.children.map {|child| child.name}.join(", ")
People, Animals, Places, Things
...
>> puts root.children[0].children.map {|child| child.name}.join(", ")
Friends, Family
...
>> Category.find_by_name('Family').parent.name
=> "People"
```

The children are dependent objects of the parents, so if you delete a parent, you'll delete the children too. Otherwise, what you've created is identical to a has_many relationship and a belongs_to relationship on category. Table 3-4 shows the methods and attributes added by the acts_as_tree relationship.

*Table 3-4. Metaprogramming for acts_as_tree*

| Added feature | Description |
| --- | --- |
| **Methods** | |
| All methods from has_many | A tree will have all of the methods of a has_many relationship, with children as the `<associations>` collection: `category.children.create` |
| **Attributes** | |
| Parent | `category.parent` |
| Children[] | An array of children: `category.children` |

# What You Haven't Seen

Active Record is too big to cover in detail in such a short book, but you should know about its major capabilities. You'll find each of these capabilities in Active Record, complete with documentation:

*Nested sets*
> Nested sets are useful for storing very large trees when you'd like to retrieve all descendents often. The nested set uses an algorithm that expresses the set as a depth-first traversal of the tree. See the Active Record documentation at *http://api.rubyonrails.com* for details.

*Overrides*
> You can declare your own accessors instead of using the ones that Active Record generates. Your new ones override those provided by `ActiveRecord::Base`.

*Versioning*
> Active Record uses the column `lock_version`, if it exists, to manage concurrency using a technique called *optimistic locking*. With this technique, a database engine can store multiple versions of each piece of data and maintain database integrity if many applications need the same piece of data.

*Count caching*
> Rather than using SQL to compute the number of certain types of objects, Active Record can cache the counts for performance.

*Timestamping*

Active Record can update timestamps when a record is created or updated.

*Enhancements*

Active Record gets new features frequently. We recommend that you periodically check the documentation and watch the various Rails mailing lists if you're going to be doing regular Rails development.

# Looking Ahead

In the first three chapters, you learned how to build models, views, and controllers. In the next few chapters, we'll continue to flesh out the Photo Share application. First, we'll use scaffolding to rapidly build the user interface. Then, we'll extend the resulting application through controllers and views. You'll have a full working application a few hours from now.

# CHAPTER 4

# Scaffolding

For centuries, scaffolding has helped builders provide access and support to buildings through the early stages of the construction process. Programmers, too, use temporary scaffolding code to lend structure and support until more permanent code is available. Rails automates scaffolding to make early coding more productive than ever before.

In almost any Ruby on Rails demonstration of five minutes or more, you're likely to see scaffolding. Rails opponents dismiss the feature quickly, saying that any scaffolding code must be thrown away, so the advantages are artificial. In some ways, the detractors are right. Scaffolding user interfaces are ugly and incomplete. But scaffolding provides more than cheap demo thrills. Here are some benefits:

- You can quickly get code in front of your users for feedback.
- You are motivated by faster success.
- You can learn how Rails works by looking at generated code.
- You can use the scaffolding as a foundation to jumpstarts your development.
- You can use metaprogramming that's automatically updated as the structure in the database changes.

In this chapter, we'll show how to use scaffolding to build a primitive user interface for Photo Share. Then, in later chapters, we will extend that foundation to flesh out our application.

## Using the Scaffold Method

We've already demonstrated a working model for Photo Share, including photos, categories, slideshows, and slides, and you should be able to manage schema from Active Record objects with the Rails console. The next step is to use scaffolding to build primitive web user interfaces for these classes. Scaffolding will take you a good ways down the road, but it won't generate a completed application. That's okay. We're looking for a head start, not a completed production-quality application.

## A List of Photos

Let's start by letting the user manage a list of photos from the Web. Ensure that you've got a database, that it's configured, and that you've got tables with model objects for slides, slideshows, categories, and photos.* If your server is not started, restart it as usual with `ruby script/server`. Point your browser to *http://localhost:3000/* to make sure things are working. You'll see the Rails welcome page if everything is working correctly. Let's build some scaffolding.

You'll start to build scaffolding using the `scaffold` method. That method goes into the controller, so we need to generate a controller called Photos:

```
ruby script/generate controller Photos
```

Add the `scaffold :photo` method to `photo_controller.rb`, like this:

```
class PhotosController < ApplicationController
  scaffold :photo
end
```

That's all you need—Rails will do the rest. Now, load the URL *http://localhost:3000/photos* to see the scaffolding in action. You'll see a list of photos, with links to create new photos, edit existing photos, and show existing photos. With the simple `scaffold :photo` statement, you got all the pages that show in Figure 4-1. The scaffolding generates surprisingly complete controller and view code. To be sure, the scaffolding does not generate production-ready code, but it's a starting point. The next section shows how scaffolding works.

 If you get the following error when trying to access the application:

```
Mysql::Error in Photo#list
Access denied for user: 'root@localhost' (Using password: NO)
```

it means that you forgot to restart the server.

## More Metaprogramming

`scaffold :photo` does the magic. `scaffold` is a method on `ActionController`.† `:photo` is a symbol that determines the Active Record model that Rails uses for this scaffold. When you specify this single method, Rails adds to your controller the nine methods in Table 4-1. Four of them render views. Together, the methods build a simple CRUD interface for your Active Record model based on the model object. Within the model, the `@@content_columns` attribute contains information about each of the columns in the database.

---

* If you haven't been coding along but wish to start, you can download all of the code through Chapter 3 from the book's web page (*http://www.oreilly.com/catalog/rubyrails*).

† You can see the actual definition in the Rails source code. `scaffold` is actually defined on `ClassMethods` and mixed in as a module to `ActionController`.

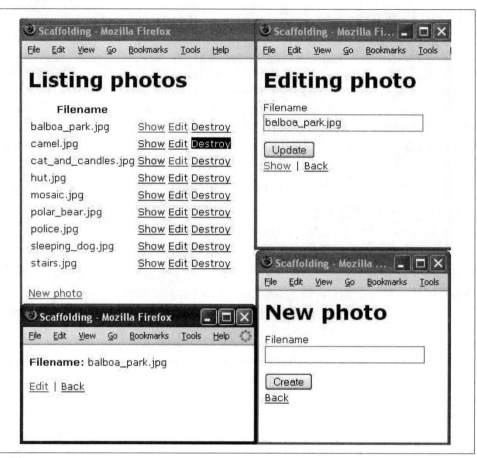

*Figure 4-1. Scaffolding renders all four of these views*

*Table 4-1. The scaffold :target method on a Rails controller creates the methods on the controller*

| Methods | Purpose | View |
|---|---|---|
| index | Renders a welcome page. By default, index redirects to the list controller action. Also, by default, when a user specifies a controller but no action, Rails invokes the index action. | No |
| list | Renders a view with a paginated list of *target* objects, in which the target object is the model object for the scaffold. | Yes |
| create(*target*) | Creates and saves an Active Record object from the target object. | No |
| new | Renders a view to create a new controller object. | Yes |
| edit(*id*) | Renders a view to edit the target object with the supplied *id*. | Yes |
| update(*id*) | Updates the active record target object with the supplied *id*. | No |
| show(*id*) | Renders a view to show an object | Yes |

*Table 4-1. The scaffold :target method on a Rails controller creates the methods on the controller (continued)*

| Methods | Purpose | View |
|---|---|---|
| destroy(id) | Destroys the object of type target with the supplied id. | No |
| render_scaffold | Renders the default view for the view methods if no .rhtml view is present. | N/A |

Most of the methods listed in Table 4-1 wind up calling the render_scaffold method, which checks to see whether you've added the corresponding view. (Remember that by default, Rails views will have the same name as the controller method.) If so, Rails uses your views. Otherwise, the controller provides default views.

# Replacing Scaffolding

In many frameworks (such as those that rely completely on code generation), once you replace any of the scaffolding, you take on responsibility for managing all of the scaffolding yourself. Not so with Rails. You can modify or rewrite any single view or controller method without affecting the rest of the scaffolding. For example, let's add a title page through the index method to the PhotosController class:

```
class PhotosController < ApplicationController
  scaffold :photo

  def index
    render_text('Welcome to Photo Share\'s Title Page')
  end
end
```

Now, load *http://localhost:3000/photos/index*. You'll see the "Welcome to Photo Share's Title Page" message printed, as in Figure 4-2, which shows that you've overridden the index method provided by the scaffolding.

*Figure 4-2. Overriding the index method*

Load *http://localhost:3000/photos/list* to verify that the rest of the scaffolding is still intact. Rails also makes it easy to replace a view while leaving the controller scaffolding intact. Let's replace the view for the show action. Create the file *app/views/photos/show.rhtml*:

```
<h1>Show Photos</h1>

<p>filename: <%= @photo.filename %></p>

<%= link_to 'list of photos', :action => 'list', :id => @photo %>
```

You'll see the view shown in Figure 4-3. As before, you can replace some views and leave the others intact. As you can see, scaffolding stays around until you need to override it. Then it just gradually melts away, a piece at a time, as you replace it.

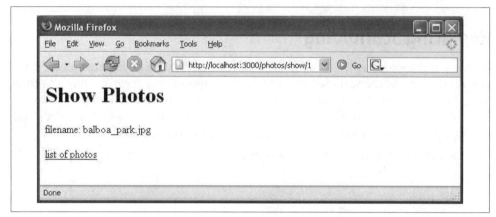

*Figure 4-3. Overriding a scaffolding view*

## Scaffolding Is Dynamic

You can use Rails scaffolding to provide a simple user interface while you're working on your database schema. Your users can then verify that you're maintaining all of the data you need. Let's see how the Rails scaffolding handles changes in the schema. We'll start by adding columns for a timestamp, a thumbnail, and a description to the photos database table. Create a new migration called *add_photo_columns* that changes the definition of the photos table by typing ruby script/generate migration add_photo_columns. Edit the resulting migration in *db/migrate* to look like this:

```
class AddPhotoColumns < ActiveRecord::Migration
  def self.up
    add_column "photos", "created_at", :datetime
    add_column "photos", "thumbnail", :string
    add_column "photos", "description", :string
    Photo.find(:all).each do |photo|
      photo.update_attribute :created_at, Time.now
      photo.update_attribute :thumbnail, photo.filename.gsub('.', '_m.')
    end
  end
end
```

```
    def self.down
      remove_column "photos", "created_at"
      remove_column "photos", "thumbnail"
      remove_column "photos", "description"
    end
  end
```

This migration script updates the photos table and the data in it. Now, execute the migration by typing rake migrate, and reload your browser (*http://localhost:3000/ photos/list*). You'll see the new columns appear, as in Figure 4-4. In fact, all of the scaffolding views work. So using scaffolding, you can quickly improve your database schema and model without having to focus on your user interface development at the same time.

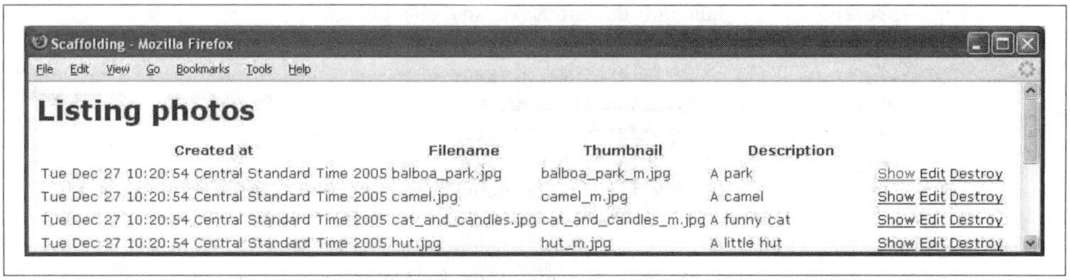

*Figure 4-4. A view created using scaffolding*

## Pros and Cons

You've just seen how to use scaffolding with the scaffold tag, or the metaprogramming approach. This approach to scaffolding has some critical advantages over other frameworks, like code generation:

- The scaffold tag is dynamic, allowing you the freedom to build on the database schema; the user interface automatically changes to keep up.

- You can override controller methods or views without having to maintain all of the scaffolding yourself.

- The scaffold tag is terse, so you can accomplish much with a single line of code.

In general, the Rails metaprogramming approach provides revolutionary advantages over code generation. Most significantly, dynamic scaffolding continually changes with the surroundings. But the metaprogramming approach does have some core disadvantages as well:

- You can't see what's going on. If you are learning Rails or scaffolding, having the code hidden from you is a distinct disadvantage.

- The behavior of the scaffolding may change with later versions of Rails. This behavior may be a distinct disadvantage if you need to maintain predictability.

- You can't use the scaffolding code as a base for further development.

For these reasons, Rails offers code generation as an alternative method for scaffolding. We'll explore the scaffolding code generator next.

# Generating Scaffolding Code

Code generation is the other major form of scaffolding. You generate scaffolding with the ruby script/generate scaffold command. Run it without parameters to see the parameters you can specify and a description of the generator:

```
> ruby script/generate scaffold
Usage: script/generate scaffold ModelName [ControllerName] [action, ...]

General Options:
    -p, --pretend      Run but do not make any changes.
    -f, --force        Overwrite files that already exist.
    -s, --skip         Skip files that already exist.
    -q, --quiet        Suppress normal output.
    -t, --backtrace    Debugging: show backtrace on errors.
    -h, --help         Show this help message.
    -c, --svn          Modify files with subversion. (Note: svn must be in path)

Description:
    The scaffold generator creates a controller to interact with a model.
    ...
```

Here, you need to specify a model and a controller name. So, to generate the scaffolding for the controller and views of our Photo model, type:

```
> ruby script/generate scaffold photo photos
  ...
```

Respond y when Rails asks if you want to replace a file. Any additional parameters are added as empty methods on the new controller. If you omit the name of the controller, Rails uses the English plural of the model name. So, to generate scaffolding for our slides, slideshows and categories, type:

```
ruby script/generate scaffold slide
...
ruby script/generate scaffold slideshow
...
ruby script/generate scaffold category
...
```

# Inside the Generated Code

Let's look at the controller Rails generated. Your version may be slightly different than the code you see here, but the principles should be the same. Open *apps/controllers/photos_controller.rb*:

```
class PhotosController < ApplicationController
  def index
    list
```

```ruby
    render :action => 'list'
  end

  def list
    @photo_pages, @photos = paginate :photos, :per_page => 10
  end

  def show
    @photo = Photo.find(params[:id])
  end

  def new
    @photo = Photo.new
  end

  def create
    @photo = Photo.new(params[:photo])
    if @photo.save
      flash[:notice] = 'Photo was successfully created.'
      redirect_to :action => 'list'
    else
      render :action => 'new'
    end
  end

  def edit
    @photo = Photo.find(params[:id])
  end

  def update
    @photo = Photo.find(params[:id])
    if @photo.update_attributes(params[:photo])
      flash[:notice] = 'Photo was successfully updated.'
```

```
      redirect_to :action => 'show', :id => @photo
    else
      render :action => 'edit'
    end
  end

  def destroy
    Photo.find(params[:id]).destroy
    redirect_to :action => 'list'
  end
end
```

As you can see, Rails generates a controller with each of the methods found in Table 4-1. Point your browser to *http://localhost:3000/photos* to verify that the generated code behaves identically to the code generated with the scaffold :photo method.

But the code is slightly different. Instead of generating the views from within the controller like the scaffold method, the generated code explicitly renders views in rhtml code. Let's look at one of the views. Open *app/views/photos/list.rhtml*:

```
1  <% for column in Photo.content_columns %>
2  <p>
3    <b><%= column.human_name %>:</b> <%=h @photo.send(column.name) %>
4  </p>
5  <% end %>
6
7  <%= link_to 'Edit', :action => 'edit', :id => @photo %> |
8  <%= link_to 'Back', :action => 'list' %>
```

This view is be rendered by the list method of PhotosController. Let's look at the first and third lines in detail:

`<% for column in Photo.content_columns %>`

In line 1, the view loops through each column in the database. Recall that Active Record added metadata to Photo, maintaining an array with each column in the table. content_columns has all of the columns that are for public display. (You don't see foreign keys or the id property, for example.)

`<b><%= column.human_name %>`

The view renders a friendly name to serve as a label of the element.

`<%=h @photo.send(column.name) %>`

The view sends a message to @photo with the name of the column and renders the result. (For example, @photo.send "filename" would be the same as @photo. filename.)

Figure 4-5 shows the result. The view lists all the properties of a Photo record in the database. The Filename property was in the database from the beginning; the Created At, Thumbnail, and Description properties were added by a migration earlier in this chapter. Furthermore, if we add more properties, the *list.rhtml* view won't require any modification to display them.

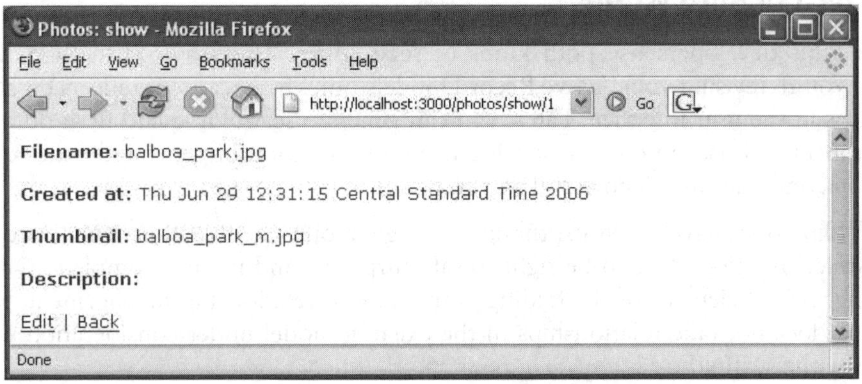

*Figure 4-5. This show view is dynamic*

The *show.rhtml* view reflects changes in the database. Now, let's look at a view that's a little less dynamic. Open *app/views/photos/_form.rhtml*:

```
<%= error_messages_for 'photo' %>

<!--[form:photo]-->
<p><label for="photo_created_at">Created at</label><br/>
<%= datetime_select 'photo', 'created_at' %></p>

<p><label for="photo_filename">Filename</label><br/>
<%= text_field 'photo', 'filename' %></p>

<p><label for="photo_thumbnail">Thumbnail</label><br/>
<%= text_field 'photo', 'thumbnail' %></p>

<p><label for="photo_description">Description</label><br/>
<%= text_field 'photo', 'description' %></p>
<!--[eoform:photo]-->
```

This view is called a partial, and it's responsible for rendering a form for a photo in *edit.rhtml* and *new.rhtml*. (You'll learn more about partials in the next chapter.) The words in bold are attributes on Photo. Because you've generated explicit code to render the form, this view works only for the database columns that were present when you created the scaffolding. So here, you see one of the primary differences between scaffolding created through metaprogramming and generated scaffolding. When we used metaprogramming, because our scaffold :photo method generated scaffolding at runtime, the scaffolding reflects changes in the database. With our generated code, the scaffolding gives a one-time benefit, but must be maintained thereafter.

## The Best of Both Worlds

Most Rails developers use both kinds of scaffolding. The scaffold method helps when you're revising your Active Record models quickly, because it reflects database changes in the user interface. Later, you can generate scaffolding and flesh out your controllers and user interfaces, starting from a foundation of generated code. Using both in combination is a powerful way to work.

Scaffolding does have its limits, though. You get a one-size-fits-all user interface and controller. It's not going to be right for all purposes, and it's not complete. One of the biggest deficiencies of scaffolding is the lack of relationship management. Scaffolding does not take relationships in the existing model under consideration when creating the scaffold.

# Moving Forward

In this chapter, we generated scaffolding for a primitive user interface. But there are limits to the scaffolding code. It doesn't manage relationships, so you can't see or edit the photos associated with a category or the slides in a slideshow. The views are also ugly and incomplete. In the next chapter, we'll start to remedy the problems. We'll use the generated scaffolding as a base and build a more complete user interface. Photo Share is moving quickly, and we're not about to slow down.

# CHAPTER 5

# Extending Views

So far, you've experienced amazing power in a short time. Rails Active Record has let you build surprisingly capable models with no more than a handful of lines of code. Scaffolding used the metaprogramming capabilities of Ruby in concert with the metadata in Active Record to instantly slap a web face on our database tables. The Rails generators and glue code kept the structure consistent and provided the necessary tools to develop and debug the application at every step of the way. Now that we have scaffolding in place for our database tables, its time to start replacing that scaffolding interface with a prettier interface—one that lets us manipulate the relationships between our tables.

This will happen faster than you might think; now the fun really begins, as our web application's user interface rapidly take shape. In this chapter, you will see how to:

- Take control of the views rendered through scaffolding
- Handle relationships in our views
- Manage layouts
- Make a simple change to Rails routing
- Manage styles

## The Big Picture

Let's step back for a moment to examine the processing steps that occur from the time the server receives a URL request to when Rails finally returns the resulting HTML response (affectionately know as *the big picture*):

1. The web server receives a request from the browser. A request consists mostly of a URL and some optional parameters (which may or may not be part of the URL).
2. The web server is normally configured to serve static resources (like images and stylesheets) directly.

3. If the URL does not match a static resource, the web server sends it to the Rails application for handling. The exact mechanism for doing this depends on both the specific web server and interface protocol that the Rails application is using (CGI, FCGI, SCGI, and so on).

4. Once the request gets delivered to the Rails application, regardless of the delivery mechanism, it is handled exactly the same way.

5. Rails parses the URL to determine the controller, action, and parameters for the request. With Rails routing, parts of the URL can specify additional parameters, and the entire routing process is under your control. Routing rules work the same on any web server because Rails controls all URL processing with the code in *config/routes.rb*, without relying on the web server.

6. The default routing (if you don't modify the routing rules) is *http://<base-url>/<controller>/<action>/<id>*. So a URL like *http://www.coolsite.com/product/order/23* calls the order method (the action) in the ProductsController class (the controller) with an id parameter set to the value 23.

7. The router calls the target action method in the target controller. The action method retrieves any needed data from any business logic in Active Record models, Action Web Services, or other backend APIs. The action method then assigns that incoming data to instance variables (like @accounts or @order). Rails automatically makes any instance variables created in the action method available to the views.

8. The action method either lets the default view template render the response, specifies a view template to render, or redirects the response to another URL. Most commonly, the action renders the default view template, which has the same name as the action.

9. Rails renders a view template to create the HTML response text that is sent back to the browser. A view template may generate the entire HTML response, but more likely is that the controller will have specified a layout template that is rendered first, with the contents of the view template being inserted into the layout. Layouts make it easy to include headers, footers, and other content that should appear on every page.

10. The view template can also cause other small templates, called *partials*, to be rendered and inserted into the view template's output. This approach is great for rendering elements than are used on more than one page or multiple times on a single page because the code won't have to be duplicated.

11. After combining the rendered output of the layout, view template, and any partials invoked by the view template, the resulting HTML response text is sent back to the browser.

Figure 5-1 shows how Rails handles an HTTP request.

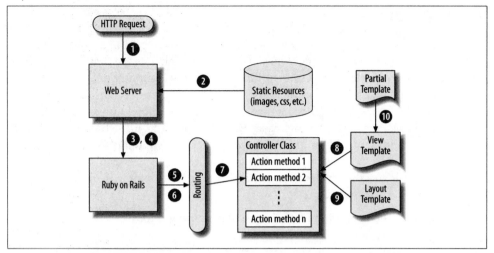

*Figure 5-1. Handling an HTTP request*

This chapter touches briefly on routing, but focuses on Steps 6 through 10. Later, we'll introduce Ajax, a richer model for building web-based user interfaces. The Ajax model will change this flow, but not by much. First, let's work on those features of Photo Share that need attention.

## Seeing Real Photos

This chapter is highly dependent on previous chapters, so if you are implementing this Photo Share application as you read, make sure that you are starting this chapter with the same source code that we have. For example, in the previous chapter, when you generated the scaffolding for each of the database tables, you could easily have let the scaffold generator overwrite the model classes in which we had specified the relationships between the tables.

The easiest way to make sure you are starting with the right code is to download our ZIP file that contains everything we have done up to this point. You can find this file on the book's web site: *http://www.oreilly.com/catalog/rubyrails*. You will want to update *config/database.yml* to specify your database configuration.

You also need some real photos to display. That same ZIP file contains sample photos, in the *public/images/photos* directory.

And, finally, make sure that your database contains the same data as ours. Use *db/create_tables_with_data.sql* to recreate the tables and data in your Photo Share database.

# View Templates

Photo Share is supposed to be a web application for storing photos, but so far the scaffolding shows only boring filenames. To make that change, we'll work with view templates and controllers. Edit the file *app/views/photos/show.rhtml*, which is the view template created by the scaffold generator. If you have used template languages like ASP or JSP* before, you will recognize the syntax for embedding executable code within the HTML template. In this case, Rails is using the *ERb* (Embedded Ruby) template system for embedding Ruby code within an HTML template. As you recall, text between <% and %> is Ruby code that is executed, text between <%= and %> is a Ruby expression, and the results from executing that code is inserted into the HTML when ERb evaluates the template.

Insert this line at the beginning of *app/views/photos/show.rhtml*:

```
<%= image_tag 'photos/' + @photo.filename %>
```

This line calls the Rails helper function image_tag, which generates an HTML <img> tag for the photo's filename. By default, images are expected to be in the *public/images* directory of our Rails app, but the photos are in *public/images/photos*, so prefix the filename with *photos/*. @photo contains the database record for the photos that we want to display and that was set by the photos controller:

```
def show
  @photo = Photo.find(params[:id])
end
```

Let's see how this looks. Make sure that the web server is started, browse to *http://127.0.0.1:3000/photos/list*, and click on the Show link for any of the pictures. Now that (Figure 5-2) is much nicer—an actual picture!

Now that you can see the images, it's time to go back and beautify the *photo/list* page. Do this by including the thumbnail image in place of the filename, and make it clickable, as a link to the *show* page. This strategy lets you eliminate almost everything else about the photo and enables the user go to the show page to see the details. Edit *app/views/photos/list.rhtml* to look like this:

```
<h1>Listing photos</h1>

<table>
<% for photo in @photos %>
  <tr>
    <td>
      <%= link_to(image_tag("photos/#{photo.thumbnail}",
                      :size => '75x56',
                      :border => 1),
               url_for(:action => 'show', :id => photo)
               )
```

---

* ASP is Microsoft's Active Server Pages, and JSP is Sun's Java Server Pages: both are HTML template systems.

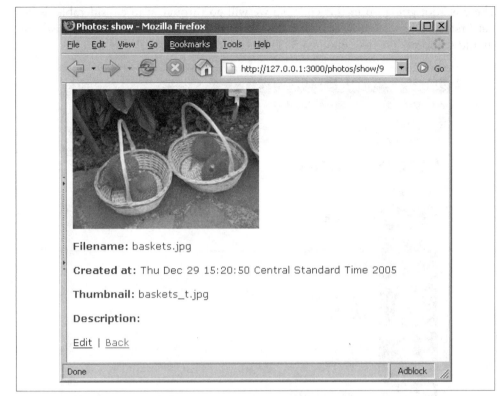

*Figure 5-2. Showing an actual photo*

```
      %>
    </td>
    <td>
      <%=h photo.filename %>
      <br/>
      <%= link_to 'delete me', { :action => 'destroy', :id => photo },
                              :confirm => 'Are you sure?' %>
    </td>
  </tr>
<% end %>
</table>

<%= link_to 'Previous page', { :page => @photo_pages.current.previous } if @photo_
pages.current.previous %>
<%= link_to 'Next page', { :page => @photo_pages.current.next } if
@photo_pages.current.next %>

<br />

<%= link_to 'New photo', :action => 'new' %>
```

There is a lot going on in this code, so we will go through it in considerable detail, but first, let's just see how it looks. Browse to *http://127.0.0.1:3000/photos/list*; you should see something like Figure 5-3. This is starting to look halfway decent.

*Figure 5-3. Thumbnails in the photo list*

Let's examine that code in detail:

```
<% for photo in @photos %>
```
Rails executes the code between <% and %>, looping through each database row contained in @photos, which contains a list of Photo objects set by the controller. Each Photo, in turn, is assigned to photo.

```
"photos/#{photo.thumbnail}"
```
Ruby allows single quotes and double quotes to delimit strings. Ruby evaluates the contents of strings with double quotes, but not single quotes. That evaluation pass will process substitutions. In this example, Ruby substitutes the result of photo.thumbnail, at execution time, for #{photo.thumbnail}, so this expression is exactly the same as 'photos/' + photo.thumbnail.

```
<%= link_to(image_tag(...), url_for(...)) %>
```
The link_to helper function creates a hyperlink. The first parameter is link text or the image to display, and the second parameter is the target URL for the link.[*]

```
image_tag("photos/#{photo.thumbnail}",
          :size => '75x56',
          :border => 1)>
```
The image_tag helper function creates an image tag. The first parameter is the path to the thumbnail, and those remaining specify attributes for the image tag.

```
url_for(:action => 'show', :id => photo)
```
The url_for helper creates a URL that targets a given controller and action. Omit the controller, so that Rails defaults to the controller invoking the view. You need the ID of the photo to show, so use the photo object. Rails will substitute the ID of that object.

```
<%=h photo.filename %>
```
The h method creates properly escaped HTML text, so characters like < become &lt;.[†] This line displays the photo's filename, making sure that any special characters are properly escaped. We could have used <%= h(photo.filename) %>, but this style is more common because it makes the h call look more like its part of the tag.

```
<%= link_to 'delete me', { :action => 'destroy', :id => photo },
                         :confirm => 'Are you sure?' %>
```
Here the link_to method is used again. This time it creates a link to the destroy method of the current controller, but with a twist. We use the :confirm option, which creates a JavaScript pop-up dialog in the browser asking "Are you sure?" If the user answers "OK," the link is taken, and the photo entry is destroyed. If the user cancels, then nothing further happens.

```
<%= link_to 'Previous page', { :page => @photo_pages.current.previous }
```
Rails supplies pagination helpers to break long lists into multiple pages with Next and Previous buttons.

```
def list
  @photo_pages, @photos = paginate :photos, :per_page => 10
end
```
This controller code, not shown in the example, calls the paginate method with two parameters. The first (:photos) says to read rows from the photos database table, and the second (:per_page => 10) says to read these rows in groups of 10.

---

[*] In Ruby, these parentheses are optional as long as the resulting code is not ambiguous. We include parentheses in this case because the parameters to link_to are themselves method calls.

[†] When you include user-entered text from the database, you want escaped text because you don't know what characters it could contain. A user could accidentally or maliciously enter text that's interpreted as a database command. Malicious attacks that enter SQL commands into text boxes are called *SQL injection attacks*.

The paginate method returns two values: @photo_pages, which captures the current page while implementing next and previous, and @photos, which is the list of database rows (photos) for the page currently in view. You'll get a previous page if one exists.

```
if @photo_pages.current.previous %>
```

Our original code creates a link to the previous page of photos (using the @photo_pages object), but only if there actually is a previous page. Ruby will conditionally executes a line if you append an if expression at the end of the line.

```
<%= link_to 'New photo', :action => 'new' %>
```

You should be able to figure this one out by now. This creates a link to the new action in the current controller.

## Layouts

You may have noticed that the HTML pages that we created are incomplete. Rails uses a feature called *layouts* to let you specify a common set of display elements for every page rendered by a controller. This feature is typically useful for common headers, footers, and sidebars. By default, Rails looks in its *app/view/layouts* directory for an RHTML file whose name matches the controller's name.

Take a look at *app/views/layouts/photos.rhtml*; you should see something like this:

```
<html>
<head>
  <title>Photos: <%= controller.action_name %></title>
  <%= stylesheet_link_tag 'scaffold' %>
</head>
<body>
  <p style="color: green"><%= flash[:notice] %></p>

  <%= @content_for_layout %>

</body>
</html>
```

This is the layout template for photos controller. The HTML output created by any action in the photos controller is inserted into the layout where you see the line:

```
<%= @content_for_layout %>
```

and sent back to the browser for display. The end result is a valid HTML page.

Let's modify this layout to add some common links that will show at the bottom of every page. Edit *app/views/layouts/photos.rhtml*, and insert the following code just before the </body> tag:

```
<div style="background-color:LightBlue">
<p>
   
  <%= link_to 'Photos', :controller => 'photos', :action => 'list' %>
```

```
 
<%= link_to 'Categories', :controller => 'categories', :action => 'list' %>
 
<%= link_to 'Slideshows', :controller => 'slideshows', :action => 'list' %>
</p>
</div>
```

This layout displays a simple navigation bar with links to the pages that list the photos, categories, and slideshows. This navigation bar appears at the bottom of every page displayed by the photos controller.

Browse to *http://127.0.0.1:3000/photos/list*; you should see a web page like the one in Figure 5-4. Try clicking the new photo link or any of the thumbnails, and notice that the navigation remains at the bottom of the page.

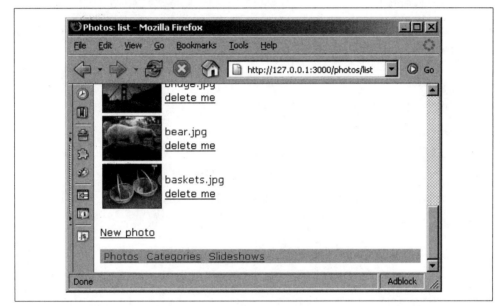

*Figure 5-4. Common navigation bar*

This navigation bar is good, but it still has a few problems. First, it appears only when you are in the photos controller. If a user clicks on the *Categories* or *Slideshows* links, the navigation will be gone. You really want the same layout to appear throughout. Second, you should move the navigation bar to the top of the page so that it doesn't seem to jump around as users move from page to page.

By default, Rails looks for a layout file with the same name as the controller, which is why we added our navigation bar in the *app/views/layouts/photos.rhtml* file. You can also tell Rails what layout file to use. We'll do that, not directly in the various controller classes, but in the common parent class for all of the controllers.

The common superclass for all of the controllers is defined in *app/controllers/application.rb*. Edit this file and add layout 'standard' to the class body so that it looks like this:

```
class ApplicationController < ActionController::Base
  layout 'standard'
end
```

This tells Rails to use a layout named "standard" instead of the default name. And putting this in the superclass is the same as putting it in each controller individually. This approach is better, of course, because you don't have to duplicate the code, and if you add a new controller in the future, it will automatically use the same layout.

Now let's create the layout template. Create *app/views/layouts/standard.rhtml* with the following content:

```
<html>
<head>
  <title>Photo Share</title>
  <%= stylesheet_link_tag 'scaffold' %>
</head>
<body>
  <div style="background-color:LightBlue">
  <p>
     
    <%= link_to 'Photos', :controller => 'photos', :action => 'list' %>
     
    <%= link_to 'Categories', :controller => 'categories', :action => 'list' %>
     
    <%= link_to 'Slideshows', :controller => 'slideshows', :action => 'list' %>
  </p>
  </div>

  <p style="color: green"><%= flash[:notice] %></p>

  <%= @content_for_layout %>

</body>
</html>
```

You probably recognize this text as pure HTML, with a few simple Ruby expressions to link to the list actions for photos, categories, and slideshows. This layout is the same as *photos.rhtml*, except that the navigation bar has been moved to the top of the page. Now you can click on any link, and every page in this Photo Share application will have this navigation bar at the top.

We no longer need the other layout files in *app/views/layouts*, so delete all of them, except for *standard.rhtml*.

# Setting the Default Root

Typing *http://127.0.0.1:3000/photos/list* or *http://localhost:3000/photos/list* is getting tedious. It would be easier to use *http://127.0.0.1:3000/* and be directed to whatever page you want to designate as the starting page. Rails handles all of the URL mapping itself, so you can easily shorten redundant URLs. *config/routes.rb* controls the routing for the application, so you need to edit this file and find this section of comments:

```
# You can have the root of your site routed by hooking up ''
# -- just remember to delete public/index.html.
# map.connect '', :controller => "welcome"
```

Now, uncomment the last line and change it to:

```
map.connect '', :controller => "photos", :action => "list"
```

With this new routing rule, any time Rails sees an empty URL (represented by the '' parameter), it should invoke the list action in the photos controller. Before this change will work, you need to delete the *public/index.html* file. If you don't, the web server will serve up *index.html* instead of *list.rhtml* whenever you browse to *http://127.0.0.1:3000/*. Because the *index.html* is static, Rails will never get called.

Now try browsing to *http://127.0.0.1:3000/*; you should see a nice new *photos/list* page, complete with thumbnails and navigation bar.

# Stylesheets

Currently, to change the styling of the application, you have to change each individual HTML element. If you've used much HTML, you know that our current design will make design work tedious and error prone. Before we get too far along beautifying our Photo Share application, we should start using stylesheets to keep all styling in one place. First, we'll create an overall application stylesheet where we will move the styles for our navigation bar and set a background color for all pages. Then we'll create a special stylesheet for specifying styles for our photos and thumbnails.

Rails creates a *scaffold.css* file that contains the basic styling used by generated scaffolding code. Let's use this as a starting point for our application's overall stylesheet. Copy the file *public/stylesheets/scaffold.css* and name this copy *public/stylesheets/application.css*.

First, change the background color to a very light gray by adding background: #eee; to the section starting body, p, ol, ul, td {. Then add a .navbar section to style the navigation bar. When you're done, the beginning of *application.css* should look like this:

```
body { background-color: #fff; color: #333; }

body, p, ol, ul, td {
```

```
    font-family: verdana, arial, helvetica, sans-serif;
    font-size:   13px;
    line-height: 18px;
    background: #eee;
}

.navbar {
  padding: 7px;
  padding-bottom: 12px;
  margin-bottom: 20px;
  background-color: LightBlue;
}

pre {
```

Now you need to edit the standard layout file (*standard.rhtml*) and replace the styling information for the navigation bar with a reference to the stylesheet. Edit *app/views/layouts/standard.rhtml* to look like this:

```
<html>
<head>
  <title>Photo Share</title>
  <%= stylesheet_link_tag 'application' %>
</head>
<body>
  <div>
  <p class="navbar">
     
    <%= link_to 'Photos', :controller => 'photos', :action => 'list' %>
     
    <%= link_to 'Categories', :controller => 'categories', :action => 'list' %>
     
    <%= link_to 'Slideshows', :controller => 'slideshows', :action => 'list' %>
  </p>
  </div>

  <p style="color: green"><%= flash[:notice] %></p>

  <%= @content_for_layout %>

</body>
</html>
```

The two changes are highlighted in bold. stylesheet_link_tag creates a link to the *application.css* file; adding class="navbar" to the paragraph tag displays it with our .navbar styles.

Let's see how this looks. If you browse to *http://127.0.0.1:3000/*; it should look like Figure 5-5.

Now let's style the photo thumbnails to have a visual frame. Create the file *public/stylesheets/photos.css* containing this:

*Figure 5-5. Using a stylesheet*

```
#thumbnail {
    padding: 1em;
    background: #ddd;
    border: thin solid #333;
}
```

Edit *app/views/layouts/standard.rhtml* and add <%= stylesheet_link_tag 'photos' %> right after the existing stylesheet tag. Then *edit app/views/photos/list.rhtml* and add an :id => 'thumbnail' attribute to the image tag. That part of *list.rhtml* should look like this:

```
<%= link_to(image_tag("photos/#{photo.thumbnail}",
                    :size => '75x56',
                    :border => 1,
                    :id => 'thumbnail'),
          url_for(:action => 'show', :id => photo)
        )
%>
```

Browse to *http://127.0.0.1:3000/* and it should look like Figure 5-6.

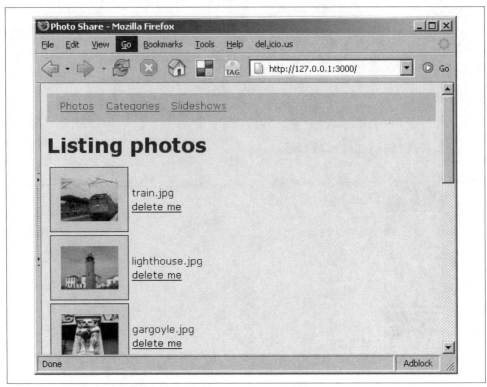

*Figure 5-6. Using a stylesheet to display borders on the pictures*

Things are starting to look pretty good.* Now we need to assign photos to categories. Also, we must be able to create and edit categories.

## Hierarchical Categories

When we generated scaffold code for categories, we got some basic CRUD screens. But they ignore the fact that our categories are hierarchical. The basic problem is every category item has a parent (except for the root category), and there is no way in the CRUD screens to specify the parent of a category.

For now, we are going to fix this in a very simple way that will get you get up and running quickly. There will be plenty of time later for a fancier user interface.

Every category has a name, but these names are not always individually unique because they are qualified by their parents in the hierarchy. For example, you might have two categories named *Car*, but one of them might have a parent named *Bruce*

---

* The borders will look a little different in Microsoft's Internet Explorer (as opposed to Firefox, shown here), due to differences in CSS handling.

while the other has a parent named *Curt*. A unique identifier for a category would prefix the category name with all of its parents. So for these two *Car* categories, we might have long names like *Root:Bruce:Car* and *Root:Curt:Car*.

Let's implement this attribute as a long_name attribute in our Category model. Edit *app/models/category.rb* to look like this (the new lines are in bold):

```ruby
class Category < ActiveRecord::Base
  has_and_belongs_to_many :photos
  acts_as_tree

  def ancestors_name
    if parent
      parent.ancestors_name + parent.name + ':'
    else
      ""
    end
  end

  def long_name
    ancestors_name + name
  end
end
```

The long_name method returns a string that is the concatenation of the names of all of its parents with its own name. ancestors_name is a recursive method that concatenates all of the parent names with a ":" separator.

You can see this working on our category list page. Edit the categories controller, *app/controllers/categories_controller.rb*, and change the list action to this:

```ruby
def list
  @all_categories = Category.find(:all, :order=>"name")
end
```

Notice that we got rid of the pagination, and that we are sorting the categories by name.

Now edit the corresponding view template, *app/views/categories/list.rhtml*, to look like this:

```erb
<h1>Listing categories</h1>

<table>
  <tr>
    <th>Name</th>
  </tr>

<% for category in @all_categories %>
  <tr>
    <td><%=h category.long_name %></td>
    <td><%= link_to 'Edit', :action => 'edit', :id => category %></td>
    <td><%= link_to 'Destroy', { :action => 'destroy', :id => category },
                                  :confirm => 'Are you sure?' %></td>
  </tr>
```

```
<% end %>
</table>

<br />

<%= link_to 'New category', :action => 'new' %>
```

The new code is in bold, and the code dealing with pagination and displaying multiple columns has been removed; plus, the *show* link was removed because the show page doesn't display anything you can't already see on the list page.

The second bolded line calls the new long_name method.

Figure 5-7 shows what you should see when you browse to *http://127.0.0.1:3000/categories/list*.

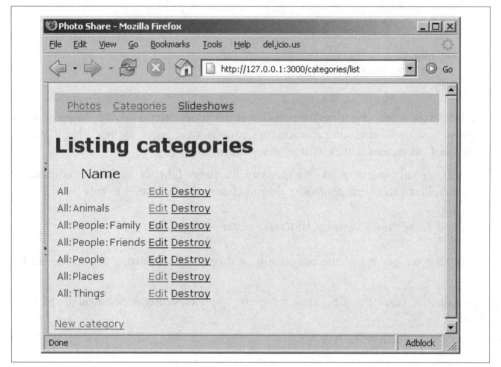

*Figure 5-7. Showing category hierarchy*

Now you need to modify creating and editing a category to let you pick the category's parent. Both actions use *app/views/categories/_form.rhtml* to display a category form, so that's the only view template you need to modify:

```
<%= error_messages_for 'category' %>

<!--[form:category]-->
<p><label for="category_name">Name</label><br/>
<%= text_field 'category', 'name'  %></p>
```

```
<p><label for="category_parent_id">Parent Category</label><br/>
<%= collection_select(:category, :parent_id,
                      @all_categories, :id, :long_name) %></p>
<!--[eoform:category]-->
```

Again, the code in bold is new. This code uses the form helper collection_select, which generates HTML <select> and <option> tags to create a drop-down select list.

The first two parameters to collection_select give the name of the database table and column whose value this control will set. The remaining three parameters specify the list of choices the user will have. @all_categories is a list of objects containing the valid choices. :id and :long_name specify the object attributes that get the key value and display value for each choice.

For this new form to work, you need to set @all_categories in the controller for the edit and new methods:

```
def new
    @category = Category.new
    @all_categories = Category.find(:all, :order=>"name")
end

...

def edit
    @category = Category.find(params[:id])
    @all_categories = Category.find(:all, :order=>"name")
end
```

Click the Edit link for any category to see the results of your handiwork (Figure 5-8).

## Assign a Category to a Photo

Let's update our photo CRUD pages so you can assign categories to a photo. For now, we will take a simple approach like we did with categories.

As with categories, both the edit photo and new photo pages use a common partial view template named _form.rhtml. As mentioned earlier, a *partial* is small template that does not render an entire page, but just a small, reusable element. This is great for rendering elements that are used on more than one page because the code won't have to be duplicated. Edit the file *app/views/photos/_form.rhtml*, and add the following to the end (just before the HTML comment):

```
<p>
  <label for="categories">Categories:</label><br/>
  <select id="categories" name="categories[]" multiple="multiple"
          size="10" style="width:250px;">
    <%= options_from_collection_for_select(@all_categories,
                                           :id, :long_name,
                                           @selected) %>
  </select>
</p>
```

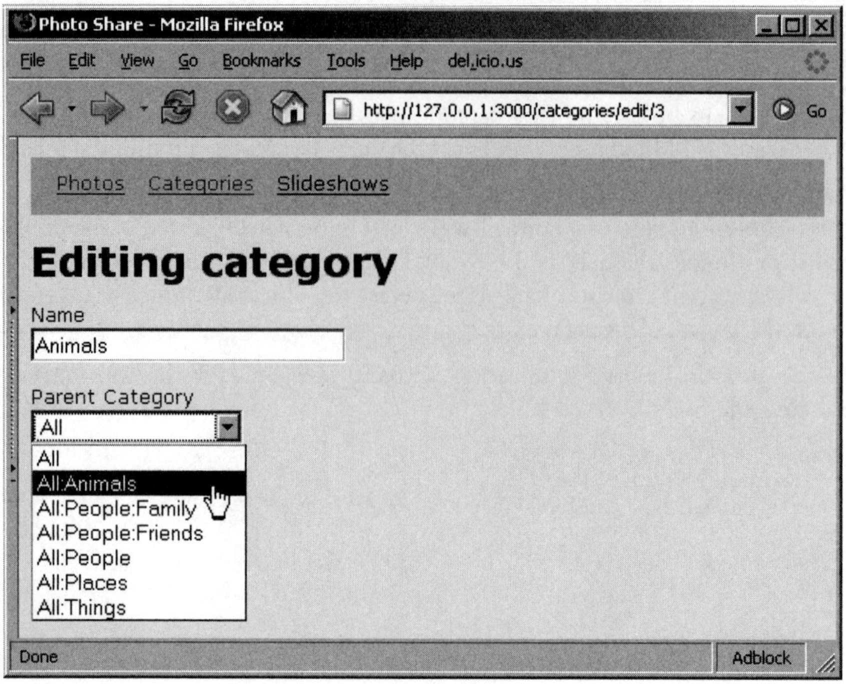

*Figure 5-8. Drop-down category selection*

This code creates a multiple-selection HTML list box populated with the category objects in the instance variable @all_categories using the id of each category as the select option's value and the long_name of each category as the select option's display text. Additionally, each category ID in @selected is displayed as already selected.

Next, you need to add code to the photos controller to set @all_categories and @selected and then grab the form results that are posted back to update the database. Edit *app/controllers/photos_controller.rb*, and change the edit and update methods to look like this (new lines are in bold):

```ruby
def edit
  @photo = Photo.find(params[:id])
  @all_categories = Category.find(:all, :order=>"name")
  @selected = @photo.categories.collect { |cat| cat.id.to_i }
end

def update
  @photo = Photo.find(params[:id])
  @photo.categories = Category.find(params[:categories]) if params[:categories]
  if @photo.update_attributes(params[:photo])
    flash[:notice] = 'Photo was successfully updated.'
    redirect_to :action => 'show', :id => @photo
  else
```

```
      render :action => 'edit'
  end
end
```

The edit method first retrieves the photo object that has the target ID and then gets a list of all categories, ordered by name. Finally, it assigns a @selected a list of IDs for all categories already assigned to this photo. @photo.categories returns a list of category objects, one for each category assigned to the photo. The Ruby collect method iterates through that list and, using the attached block of code, creates a new list consisting of just the category IDs (cat.id) converted to an integer (cat.id.to_i).

When the user saves changes to the edited photo, the form data is directed to the update method. params[:categories] contains a list of the selected categories (or nil if no categories were selected). The new if modifier we just added to the update method prevents the line from being executed when there are no selected categories.

Category.find(params[:categories]) returns a list of category objects, one for each category ID in params[:categories]. This category list is then assigned to the target photo's categories attribute.

Let's now make a very similar set of changes to the new and create methods. The only difference is that a new photo doesn't have any existing selected categories, so the @selected variable is not set:

```
def new
  @photo = Photo.new
  @all_categories = Category.find(:all, :order=>"name")
  @selected = []
end

def create
  @photo = Photo.new(params[:photo])
  @photo.categories = Category.find(params[:categories]) if params[:categories]
  if @photo.save
    flash[:notice] = 'Photo was successfully created.'
    redirect_to :action => 'list'
  else
    @all_categories = Category.find(:all, :order=>"name")
    render :action => 'new'
  end
end
```

Again, the new lines are bold.

That's all there is to it. You can now assign multiple categories to each photo. Give it a try! You should be starting to see how easy it is to incrementally build out your Photo Share application.

# Styling the Slideshows

Now that you've implemented a complex relationship, it's time to spice things up a bit. Let's take stock of where we are with the Photo Share application:

- We have created a common layout that displays navigation links on every page to the three major areas: photos, categories, and slideshows.
- The pages that deal with photos look pretty good.
- The pages that deal with categories are functional, but could use some improvement.
- We're using cascading stylesheets to specify the visual styling of our pages and their elements.

We haven't yet done anything with the slideshows, which are still using the generated scaffolding. The page that displays a list of all slideshows is the focal point that links to all the things you can do with slideshows: create them, edit them, delete them, and play them. Fixing up this page will have the tremendous visual impact, so this is a good place to start.

Currently, the list slideshows page looks like Figure 5-9. This is definitely ugly!

Figure 5-10 shows how it should look when we're done.

In the process of getting to this goal, you will learn about many new features. At the moment we've defined only one slideshow, but later on you can create more slideshows.

The slideshow controller's list action already gets the needed information from the database, so you don't need to modify *app/controllers/slideshows_controller.rb*. The list method looks like this:

```
def list
  @slideshow_pages, @slideshows = paginate :slideshows, :per_page => 10
end
```

You'll want to use the @slideshows instance variable in your view template because it contains a list of Slideshow objects to display. You've seen this code before; it is used (in this case) to break up long lists of slideshows into bite-sized chunks.

Edit the view template (*app/views/slideshows/list.rhtml*) to make it look like this:

```
<div id="slideshow-summaries">
    <% for slideshow in @slideshows %>
        <div id="slideshow-summary">
            <div id='slideshow-caption'>
                <%= slideshow.name %>
                <small>(<%= slideshow.slides.size %> slides)</small>
            </div>

            <div id="slideshow-thumbnails">
                <%= thumbnail_tag slideshow.slides[0] %>
                <%= thumbnail_tag slideshow.slides[1] %>
```

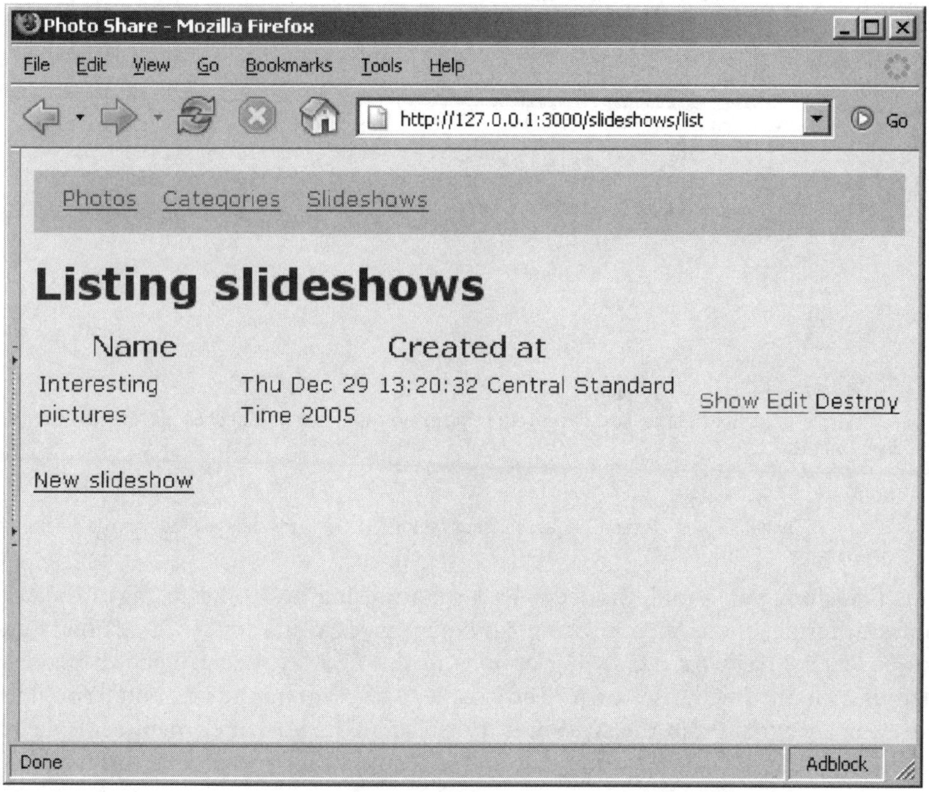

Figure 5-9. Current (ugly) slideshow listing

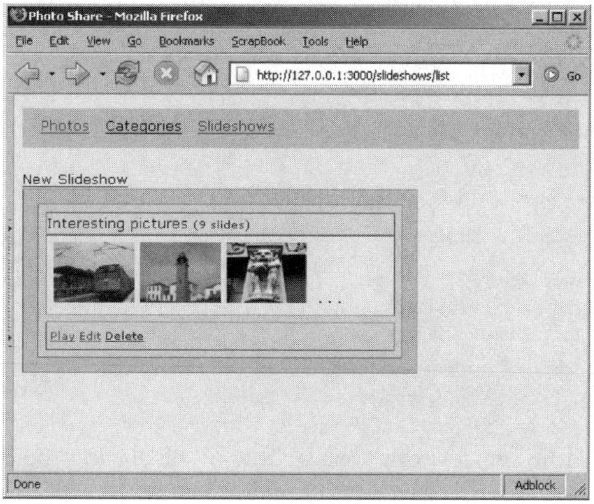

Figure 5-10. Better-looking slideshow listing

```
      <%= thumbnail_tag slideshow.slides[2] %>
       <strong>. . .</strong>
    </div>

    <div id="slideshow-controls">
      <small>
        <%= link_to 'Play',    :action => 'show',    :id => slideshow %>
        <%= link_to 'Edit',    :action => 'edit',    :id => slideshow %>
        <%= link_to 'Delete',  :action => 'destroy', :id => slideshow %>
      </small>
    </div>
  </div>
  <br/>
<% end %>

<%= link_to 'Previous page',
    { :page => @slideshow_pages.current.previous } if @slideshow_pages.current.
previous %>

<%= link_to 'Next page',
    { :page => @slideshow_pages.current.next } if @slideshow_pages.current.next %>
</div>
```

This first thing you should notice is that we are using nested <div> tags instead of tables to format the contents. Using <div> tags gives you a lot more flexibility and power when specifying the styling options in the CSS stylesheet. Each display element is contained within its own <div> section with a unique id attribute. You'll use these same div names in the stylesheet to determine how each element is displayed. We'll create the stylesheet shortly, but first let's go through the code in this template:

```
<% for slideshow in @slideshows %>
```

You saw this line before in the photos list template. It loops through each database row contained in @slideshows (which was set by the controller), assigning each, in turn, to slideshow:

```
<div id='slideshow-caption'>
  <%= slideshow.name %>
  <small>(<%= slideshow.slides.size %> slides)</small>
</div>
```

This div is simply a caption block that displays the name of the slideshow along with the number of photos it contains:

```
<div id="slideshow-thumbnails">
  <%= thumbnail_tag slideshow.slides[0] %>
  <%= thumbnail_tag slideshow.slides[1] %>
  <%= thumbnail_tag slideshow.slides[2] %>
   <strong>. . .</strong>
</div>
```

This div shows a little preview of the slideshow by displaying the thumbnails of the first three photos in the slideshow:

```
<div id="slideshow-controls">
  <small>
    <%= link_to 'Play',   :action => 'show',    :id => slideshow %>
    <%= link_to 'Edit',   :action => 'edit',    :id => slideshow %>
    <%= link_to 'Delete', :action => 'destroy', :id => slideshow %>
  </small>
</div>
```

Once again, this div should be self-explanatory. It displays a block of links for operating on this particular slideshow. It includes links to play, edit, and delete the slideshow.

When you try to list slideshows, this code breaks. Rails does not have a helper function to display thumbnails, but we'll remedy that next.

## Creating Your Own Helper Functions

Rails has many built-in helper functions to assist in creating the HTML that is sent back to the browser, and we have used many of them in our Photo Share application. You can also create your own helper functions.

You can create two kinds of helper functions. Helper functions that you want to be accessible from any controller or view template are application-level helper functions; they go in the file *app/helpers/application_helper.rb*. Helper functions that are specific to a particular controller go in *app/helpers/<controller-name>_helper.rb*.

We need to implement the thumbnail_tag helper that we used earlier. Because it's specific to the slideshows_controller, we'll add it to *app/helpers/slideshows_helper. rb*. All views rendered by the slideshows_controller will be able to use this helper. Edit *app/helpers/slideshows_helper.rb*, and add the following code inside the module definition:

```
def thumbnail_tag(slide)
  image_tag "photos/#{slide.photo.thumbnail}" if slide
end
```

The meat of the method calls the built-in helper function image_tag, passing the path to the slide's thumbnail, thus creating the proper image tag. You may have noticed that the view code assumes that there are at least three slides in a slideshow. Because some slideshows may be shorter, you need to allow for nil, so add the if slide modifier at the end. Because nil evaluates to false, execute this line of code only if you're given a slide.

## Creating the Stylesheet

Remember that we set up our view template with id= attributes: for example, "slideshow-summary" and "slideshow-thumbnails". This organization lets you create matching entries in your stylesheet to specify their display attributes.

First, let's see what the Slideshows Listing page looks like *before* you create the stylesheet. Then you'll really appreciate how easily a stylesheet can improve the look of your page. Make sure the server is started and browse to *http://127.0.0.1:3000/ slideshows/list*; you should see something like Figure 5-11.

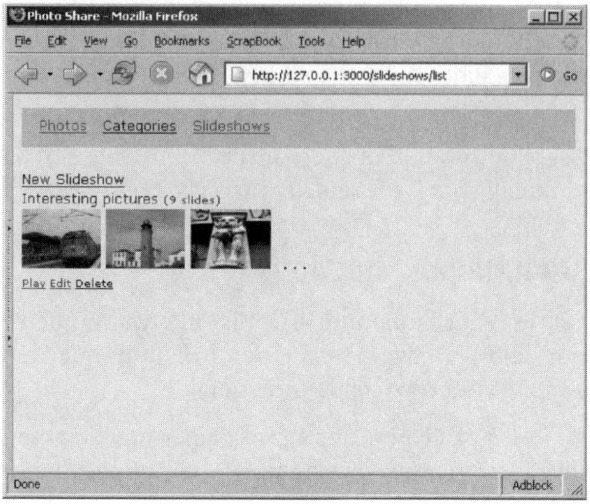

*Figure 5-11. Before stylesheet*

This page is definitely nicer than the earlier version but not as nice as it could be. Now let's create the stylesheet. Create the file *public/stylesheets/slideshows.css* with the following contents:

```
#slideshow-summaries {
    padding: 0.5em;
    float: left;
    background: #ccc;
    margin-left: auto;
    margin-right: auto;
    border-left: thin solid #777;
    border-bottom: thin solid #777;
    border-top: thin solid #aaa;
    border-right: thin solid #aaa;
}

#slideshow-summary {
    padding: 0.5em;
    margin: 0.5em;
    width: 25em;
    float: left;
    background: #ddd;
    border-left: thin solid #777;
    border-bottom: thin solid #777;
```

```
    border-top: thin solid #aaa;
    border-right: thin solid #aaa;
}

#slideshow-thumbnails {
    padding: 0.50em;
    background: #eee;
    border-left: thin solid #aaa;
    border-bottom: thin solid #aaa;
    border-top: thin solid #777;
    border-right: thin solid #777;
}

#slideshow-caption {
    background: #edd;
    border-left: thin solid #aaa;
    border-bottom: thin solid #aaa;
    border-top: thin solid #777;
    border-right: thin solid #777;
    font-size: 1.0em;
}

#slideshow-controls {
    margin-top: 0.50em;
    padding: 0.25em;
    border-left: thin solid #777;
    border-bottom: thin solid #777;
    border-top: thin solid #aaa;
    border-right: thin solid #aaa;
}
```

For the most part, these style definitions just set borders and background shading. For Rails to be able to find the stylesheet, you must include a reference to this stylesheet in your HTML pages. Edit *app/views/layouts/standard.rhtml*, and insert:

```
<%= stylesheet_link_tag 'slideshows' %>
```

immediately after the other stylesheet references.

Now, if you refresh your browser, you should see something like Figure 5-12.

That's much better. We still need to implement the ability to create, edit, and play a slideshow. We'll tackle these in the next chapter because we're going to use Rails's built-in Ajax facilities to create an intuitive Ajax user interface. In the next chapter, we'll focus on using Ajax to make this user interface more interactive, dynamic, and exciting.

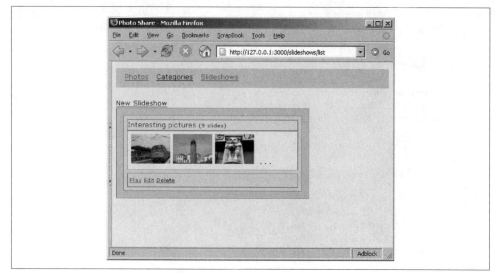

*Figure 5-12. After stylesheet*

# CHAPTER 6

# Ajax

Ajax is one of the most important emerging trends in web applications. Web sites like Google Maps and Gmail dramatically demonstrate that web applications do not have to be slow, clunky, page-at-a-time web forms. Ajax techniques can reclaim some of the fluidity and responsiveness that was lost when we moved from desktop applications to web applications.

Ajax (which stands for the cryptic "Asynchronous JavaScript and XML") is a technique for building web pages that are more interactive, exciting, and dynamic. Ajax is asynchronous: JavaScript libraries can communicate with the server at any time, and the web page need not be frozen while waiting for a response. Ajax uses JavaScript on the browser, any language on the server, and XML to specify messages.

When you use this emerging technique, a web page can communicate with the server at any time, updating only those portions of the display that need it. Users experience more responsive web pages, with immediate feedback. Even though using Ajax techniques usually requires significantly more sophisticated design and implementation skills, the benefits to the end user are so great that Ajax-enabled web applications will soon become the rule, not the exception. Fortunately, Rails makes Ajax so simple that, for typical cases, using Ajax is almost as easy as not using it.

## How Rails Implements Ajax

Rails has a simple, consistent model for how it implements Ajax operations. Once the browser has rendered and displayed the initial web page, different user actions cause it to display a new web page (like any traditional web application) or trigger an Ajax operation:

*Some trigger fires*

> This trigger could be the user clicking on a button or link, the user making changes to the data on a form or in a field, or just a periodic trigger (based on a timer).

*The web client calls the server*
> A JavaScript method, `XMLHttpRequest`, sends data associated with the trigger to an action handler on the server. The data might be the ID of a checkbox, the text in an entry field, or a whole form.

*The server does something*
> The server-side action handler—a Rails controller action (for our purposes)—does something with the data and returns an HTML fragment to the web client.

*The client receives the response*
> The client-side JavaScript, which Rails creates automatically, receives the HTML fragment and uses it to update a specified part of the current page's HTML, often the content of a `<div>` tag.

These steps are the simplest way to use Ajax in a Rails application, but with a little extra work, you can have the server return any kind of data in response to an Ajax request, and you can create custom JavaScript in the browser to perform more involved interactions. We'll stick to HTML fragments in this chapter.

Rails uses the *Prototype* and *script.aculo.us* JavaScript libraries to implement browser support for Ajax. You can use these libraries independently of Rails, but with their seamless integration with Rails, you probably won't want to. Throughout this chapter, we'll exploit the Ajax and special-effects capabilities that come with Rails to implement missing features in our Photo Share application.

# Playing a Slideshow

Let's see what happens when we try to play a slideshow. Browse to *http://127.0.0.1:3000/slideshows/list*, and click the Play link for our only slideshow. As you can see in Figure 6-1, this URL invokes the *show* action on the *slideshow* controller, but the action is still using the scaffold code.

We need to change this page to actually "play" the slideshow by sequentially displaying the pictures contained in the slideshow. To do this, we will initially display the first picture in the slideshow; then, once every two seconds, we'll make an Ajax call to get and display the next picture.

The controller sets up all the slides in a slideshow for playback. You need to start `@slideshow` with the current slideshow set to play. You also need to put the current slide (initially, 0) and the whole slideshow into a holding area called the *session*, so you won't have to read from the database each time you play a new slide. Edit the slideshows controller (*app/controllers/slideshows_controller.rb*), and modify the show method to look like this:

```
def show
  @slideshow = Slideshow.find(params[:id])
  session[:slideshow] = @slideshow
  session[:slide_index] = 0
```

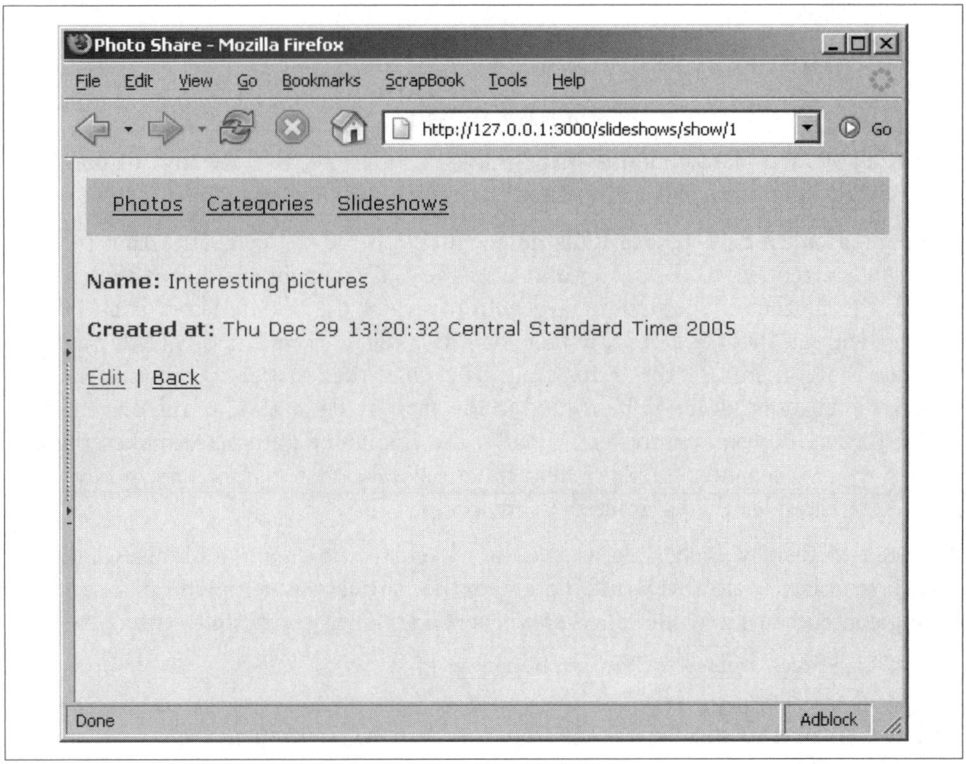

*Figure 6-1. Playing a slideshow that still uses scaffolding*

```
    @slide = @slideshow.slides[0]
end
```

Every two seconds in this code, the browser sends an Ajax request to get the next slide. You can't use instance variables to keep track of where you are in the slideshow because instance variables exist only until you finish processing the current request. Use the Rails-provided session object instead, which is persistent across requests. Let's look at this code in a little more detail.

`session[:slideshow] = @slideshow` stores a reference to the current slideshow in the session hash at the key `:slideshow`. We do the same thing with the index of the current slide that is being played. We initially set the `slide_index` to zero to point to the first slide, and our Ajax request increments the index by one as it displays each slide. We can retrieve these values from the session hash during the Ajax requests for the next slide.

Now, edit the view template (*app/views/slideshows/show.rhtml*) to look like this:

```
<p><i><%= @slideshow.name %></i></p>

<div id="slides">
  <%= render :partial => "show_slide" %>
```

```
    </div>

    <%= periodically_call_remote :update    => 'slides',
                                 :url       => { :action => :show_slide },
                                 :frequency => 2.0 %>
```

This RHTML template contains three things: a title line, the div that displays the current slide, and a magic Ajax incantation that we will now pick apart.

The periodically_call_remote Rails helper function creates JavaScript that periodically sends a request to the server and uses the HTML fragment that is returned to replace the content of the update target. In this case, the update target is an HTML element with an ID of 'slides', which is a <div> tag. The returned HTML fragment replaces the contents of this <div> tag. The URL that makes the request is constructed to ensure that it will be routed to the show_slide method of the current controller (the slideshows controller). Finally, the frequency parameter makes the call once every two seconds. All Ajax help functions take their parameters in key/value pairs, so you can list the parameters in any order.

We need to display each slide as it comes back to the client; Rails uses a partial HTML template to do this work. To create the partial view template, place the following contents in a new file called *app/views/slideshows/_show_slide.rhtml*:

```
    <%= image_tag "photos/#{@slide.photo.filename}" %>
    <p><%= @slide.photo.filename %></p>
```

And its controller method in *app/controllers/slideshows_controller.rb*:

```
    def show_slide
      @slideshow = session[:slideshow]
      session[:slide_index] += 1
      @slide = @slideshow.slides[session[:slide_index]]
      if @slide == nil
        session[:slide_index] = 0
        @slide = @slideshow.slides[0]
      end
      render :partial => "show_slide"
    end
```

This method retrieves the slideshow information from the session, moves to the next slide (or back to the beginning if at the end), and then explicitly renders the partial view template show_slide. You need to render a partial view or render with the option :render_layout => false. Otherwise, Rails tries to render a full template, including layout. As our page already has a layout, simply render a partial template, consisting of an image tag for the slide, and its name.

Finally, you need to update your standard layout template to include script tags for the Prototype JavaScript library because the client-side JavaScript code that Rails creates for you uses them, so in *app/views/layouts/standard.rhtml*, insert this line immediately after the title tags:

```
    <%= javascript_include_tag 'prototype', 'effects', 'dragdrop' %>
```

This line includes three JavaScript files that are shipped with Rails: *prototype.js* and two *Script.aculos.us* files, *effects.js* and *dragdrop.js*. We will use these last two shortly.

Now show a slideshow by loading *slideshows/list* and clicking Show, and you will see the actual pictures in the slideshow, changing every two seconds.

# Using Drag-and-Drop to Reorder Slides

The scaffolding we have for editing a slideshow shows just the slideshow attributes that are stored directly in the *slideshows* table: the slideshow's name and the date on which it was created. The most important part is missing: the photos that are part of the slideshow!

By now, you've probably realized that this is because the scaffolding code deals with only one database table: the *slideshows* table. The relationship data about which photos are assigned to a slideshow and their order in the slideshow are stored in the *slides* table. Scaffolding does not handle relationships, so you have to write the code to edit this relationship data.

We're going to display a list of thumbnails of all the photos that are in a slideshow, and then let the user reorder them using drag-and-drop. If you've had to struggle through implementing drag-and-drop before, you're not going to believe how easy this is going to be. Here's a hint: this will take a total 34 additional lines of Ruby, CSS, and RHTML template!

Let's start by reviewing the current implementation of the edit action in the slideshow controller:

```
def edit
  @slideshow = Slideshow.find(params[:id])
end
```

This action expects to find the ID of the slideshow to edit passed in as the id parameter, which is normally decoded from the URL. You find the slideshow with that ID and assign that slideshow object to the instance variable @slideshow, so that it can be accessed in the view template.

That is really all that's needed here, so you won't have to add any code to this method. The changes will start with the edit view template, so edit the template *photos/app/views/slideshows/edit.rhtml* and make it look like this (the changes are in bold):

```
<h1>Editing slideshow</h1>

<%= link_to 'Play this Slideshow',
            :action => 'show', :id => @slideshow %>

<div id='slideshow-contents'>
  <%= render :partial => 'show_slides_draggable' %>
</div>
```

```
<div id='slideshow-attributes'>
  <%= start_form_tag :action => 'update', :id => @slideshow %>
    <%= render :partial => 'form' %>
    <%= submit_tag 'Save Attributes' %>
  <%= end_form_tag %>
</div>
```

Notice that the existing <%= render :partial => 'form' %> is wrapped in a <div> tag with an id attribute of slideshow-attributes. You will use this name in one of your CSS files to control how this section is displayed.

There is also a completely new section that displays thumbnails of the photos in the slideshow:

```
<div id='slideshow-contents'>
  <%= render :partial => 'show_slides_draggable' %>
</div>
```

This code also uses a <div> tag with an id attribute, for the same reason: to use a CSS file to control its appearance. This div also renders a new partial view template named show_slides_draggable, which we will create next.

Create the file *photos/app/views/slideshows/_show_slides_draggable.rhtml* with the following contents:

```
<ol id='sortable_thumbs'>
  <% for slide in @slideshow.slides %>
    <li id='thumbs_<%= slide.id %>' class='slides'>
      <%= thumbnail_tag slide %>
    </li>
  <% end %>
</ol>

<%= sortable_element('sortable_thumbs',
                     :url => {:action => 'update_slide_order'}) %>
```

The first part is pretty standard stuff. We're creating an HTML ordered list, in which each list item is a thumbnail image of one of the photos in the slideshow (note that the thumbnail_tag helper function that was created earlier). However, it's the last two lines that do the heavy lifting.

sortable_element is a helper function that generates the JavaScript code that turns our list into a user-sortable, drag-and-drop-capable list. It wraps this list an HTML form, and the :url option specifies the URL to post to the server whenever the user changes the order of the list. In this case, it calls the action method update_slide_order in our slideshow controller. This call works in the background using an Ajax call.

The update_slide_order method is pretty simple as well. Edit *photos/app/controllers/slideshows_controller.rb*, and add this method:

```
def update_slide_order
  params[:sortable_thumbs].each_with_index do |id, position|
```

```
      Slide.update(id, :position => position)
    end
  end
```

This method iterates through each slide in the list, extracting its ID and position in the list, and uses this information to update that slide's database row with its new position. Let's walk through this code in a little more detail:

- params is a hash that holds all the parameters sent to the server in the HTTP request. params[:sortable_thumbs] retrieves the parameter for the sortable_thumbs list, which is an ordered array of the IDs of each thumbnail in the list.

- each_with_index is a Ruby iterator that, just like the each iterator, walks through the array one item at a time. But on each iteration, each_with_index passes to the code block both the object held in the array (the slide id) and its index in the array (which is assigned to position).

- Slide.update(id, :position => position) then calls the Slide model class to update the slide identified by id with its new position.

We're almost ready to give it a try, but first let's edit *photos/public/stylesheets/slideshows.css* and add some formatting instructions for the two div IDs we created. Add the following at the end of the file:

```
#slideshow-contents {
    float: left;
    width: 11em;
    padding: 0.50em;
    text-align: center;
    border-right: thin solid #bbb;
    padding: 0.50em;
    padding-bottom: 10em;
}

#slideshow-attributes {
    margin-left: 23em;
    padding-left: 1.5em;
    padding-top: 1.5em;
}
```

This causes the contents of the slideshow (which will be a list of thumbnail images) to be displayed down the left side of the page, and the slideshow's attributes will be displayed immediately to the right of the thumbnails.

Let's see how this looks. Browse to *http://127.0.0.1:3000/slideshows/list*, and click the edit link for our one and only slideshow. It will look like Figure 6-2.

Click on one of the photos, and try dragging it around. When you drop it into a new location, update_slide_order is called to write the new order to the database.

Let's fix one minor thing here before we move on. Wouldn't it be better to see the number of each photo appear vertically aligned in the middle of the thumbnail instead of at the bottom? Because the HTML for each thumbnail image is created by

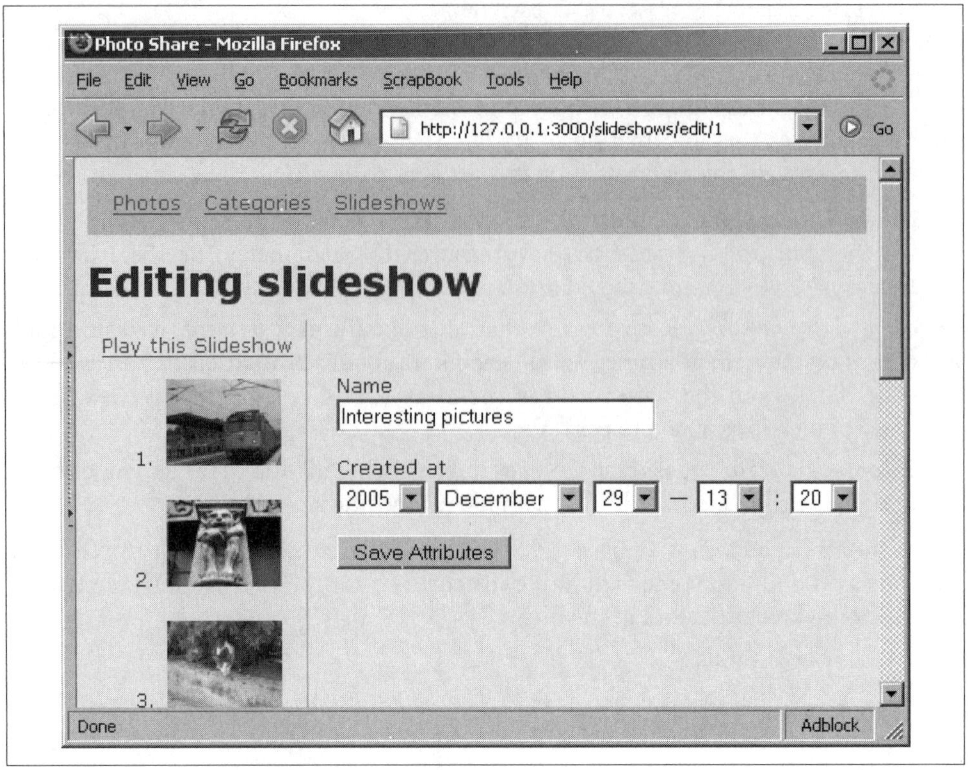

*Figure 6-2. A drag-and-drop list of photos*

our own helper function, `thumbnail_tag`, we just need to edit that function and add a vertical-align style attribute.

First, edit *photos/app/helpers/slideshows_helper.rb*, and add the code shown in bold:

```
module SlideshowsHelper
  def thumbnail_tag(slide)
    image_tag("photos/#{slide.photo.thumbnail}",
           :style=>"vertical-align:middle") if slide
  end
end
```

Now, refresh your browser: the list numbers are nicely centered, as you can see in Figure 6-3.

With a very small amount of code, we added a very nice drag-and-drop user interface for reordering the slides in a slideshow. But we're just getting started with our Ajax-enabled user interface.

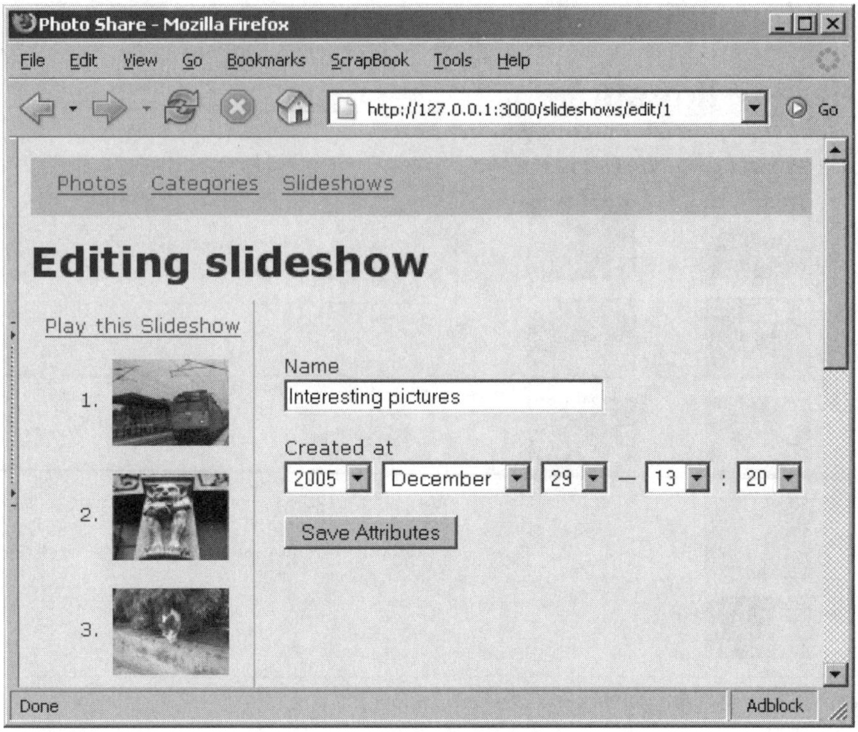

*Figure 6-3. Nicely centered list numbers*

# Drag and Drop Everything (Almost Everything)

We have already displayed a list of thumbnails of all photos that are in the slideshow and enabled the user to drag them around to rearrange their order in the slideshow. Now let's add a second list of thumbnails, showing all photos that are not being used in the slideshow.

We'll let the user add a photo to the slideshow by dragging it from the list of unused photos and dropping it onto the slideshow thumbnails. Similarly, we can enable the user to remove photos from the slideshow by dragging its thumbnail from the slideshow and dropping on the unused photos list. Finally, we'll allow the user to filter the unused photos list by category.

As you might expect, we can accomplish all that in a very small amount of code. We will add a mere 58 lines of Ruby code to the models and controllers, 47 lines to the view templates, and 16 lines to our CSS stylesheet! Figure 6-4 gives you a preview of how this is going to look when we're done.

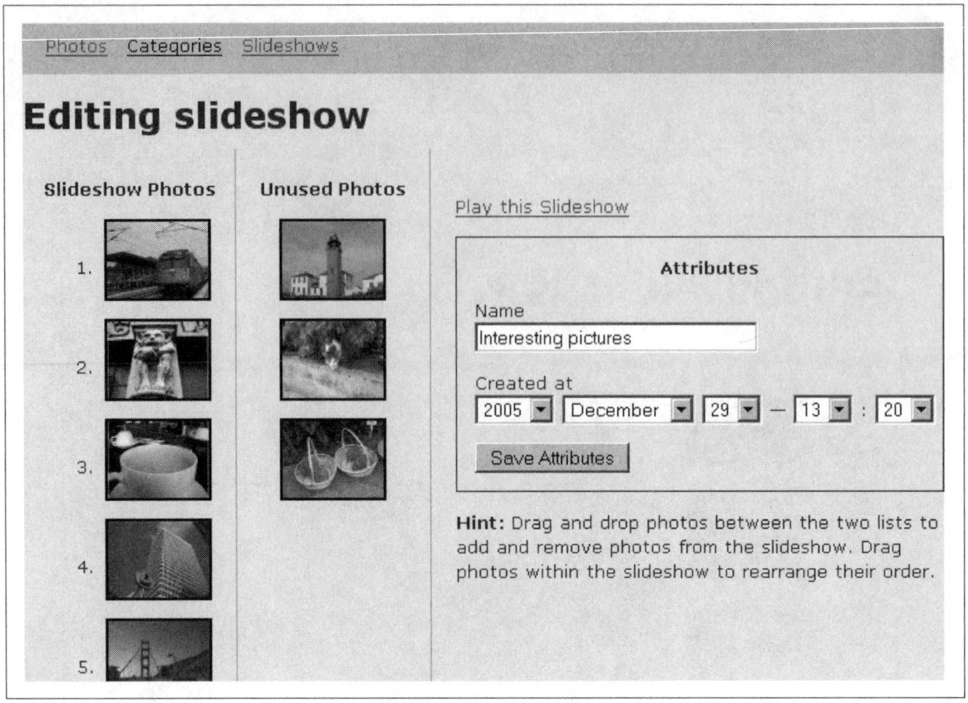

Figure 6-4. Preview of drag-and-drop slideshow editing

Let's start by updating the slideshow's edit template. Edit *photos/app/views/slideshows/edit.rhtml* to look like this:

```
<h1>Editing slideshow</h1>

<div id='slideshow-contents'>
  <p style='text-align: center;'><b>Slideshow Photos</b></p>
  <div id='slideshow-thumbs'>
    <%= render :partial => 'show_slides_draggable' %>
  </div>
</div>

<div id='slideshow-photo-picker'>
  <p style='text-align: center;'><b>Unused Photos</b></p>
  <div id='slideshow-photos'>
    <%= render :partial => 'photo_picker' %>
  </div>
</div>

<div id='slideshow-attributes'>
  <p><%= link_to 'Play this Slideshow', :action => 'show', :id => @slideshow %></p>
  <div style='border: thin solid; padding-left: 1em;'>
    <p style='text-align: center;'><b>Attributes</b></p>
    <%= start_form_tag :action => 'update', :id => @slideshow %>
      <%= render :partial => 'form' %>
```

```
          <%= submit_tag 'Save Attributes' %>
        <%= end_form_tag %>
    </div>
    <p>
      <b>Hint:</b> Drag and drop photos between the
      two lists to add and remove photos from the
      slideshow. Drag photos within the slideshow to
      rearrange their order.
    </p>
  </div>

  <%= drop_receiving_element("slideshow-contents",
          :update => "slideshow-thumbs",
          :url => {:action => "add_photo" },
          :accept => "photos",
          :droponempty => "true",
          :loading => visual_effect(:fade),
          :complete => visual_effect(:highlight, 'sortable_thumbs')
          ) %>
```

This file has been almost entirely rewritten, so there are no marked-as-changed lines. You can see that I have laid out this edit page into three sections:

```
<div id='slideshow-contents'> . . . </div>
<div id='slideshow-photo-picker'> . . . </div>
<div id='slideshow-attributes'> . . . </div>
```

Only the slideshow-photo-picker is new. It shows the list of unused photos that can be added to the slideshow. We will set up the CSS stylesheet to display these sections side-by-side as you saw them in Figure 6-4.

slideshow-contents is rendered by the partial template show_slides_draggable, slideshow-photo-picker is rendered by the partial template photo_picker, and slideshow-attributes is mostly rendered by the form partial template that was generated from the scaffolding. I say "mostly" because I added a few things inline around the rendering of form.

Finally, notice two Ajax related helpers: drop_receiving_element and observe_field. We'll come back to these in a little bit after we have discussed some prerequisite details.

Now, make these changes to *photos/app/controllers/slideshows_controller.rb*, replacing the edit method and creating the unused_photos method:

```
def edit
  @slideshow = Slideshow.find(params[:id])
  session[:slideshow] = @slideshow
  @photos = unused_photos(@slideshow)
end

def unused_photos(slideshow)
  all_photos = Photo.find(:all)
  candidates = []
```

```
    for photo in all_photos
        in_slideshow = false
        for slide in slideshow.slides
            if slide.photo.thumbnail === photo.thumbnail
                in_slideshow = true
                break
            end
        end
        candidates << photo if not in_slideshow
    end
    return candidates
end
```

The purpose of this code is to retrieve all the data needed by the *edit.rhtml* view template:

`@slideshow = Slideshow.find(params[:id])`

The id of the slideshow that you want to edit is passed in the request parameters from the browser. Here you retrieve that id and read that slideshow from the database, which you store in the instance variable @slideshow to make it available to the view template.

`session[:slideshow] = @slideshow`

Ajax actions requests will be coming in as the user makes changes, and you need to know what slideshow to change. This line saves a reference to the slideshow in the session hash. I'm using a key value of :slideshow to save and retrieve this from the session, but that value is arbitrary and could have been any unique identifier.

`@photos = unused_photos(@slideshow)`

This line calls the new method unused_photos to retrieve a list of all photos that are not in the slideshow; it then saves that list in @photos.

`def unused_photos(slideshow)`

This method returns a list of photos that are not in the slideshow. The logic should be self-explanatory. First, create an empty array (candidates = []), and then iterate through the list of all photos, adding them to the array (candidates << photo) if they are not already in the slideshow. The technique used here is grossly inefficient, but it will suffice for our purposes.

We still need to create the *photo_picker* template that generates the HTML to display all the photos that can still be added to a slideshow, so go ahead and create the file *photos/app/views/slideshows/_photo_picker.rhtml* with this in it:

```
<% for photo in @photos %>
    <%= image_tag("photos/#{photo.thumbnail}",
                    :style => "vertical-align: middle",
                    :id => "photo_#{photo.id}",
                    :class => "photos") %>
    <%= draggable_element "photo_#{photo.id}", :revert => true %>
<% end %>
```

This template iterates through the list of photos in @photos. For each photo, it uses the image_tag helper to create an HTML image tag and the draggable_element helper to generate the JavaScript code that makes it draggable. You can see that the first parameter of draggable_element matches the value of the id attribute (:id => "photo_ #{photo.id}") on the image tag. The draggable_element helper expects the id of the HTML element that it should make draggable, followed by zero or more options. The single option used here (:revert => true) says to move the element back to its original position after it is dropped.

But where can these draggable images be dropped? Recall that at the end of the slide-show's *edit.rthtml* template we had:

```
<%= drop_receiving_element("slideshow-contents",
        :update => "slideshow-thumbs",
        :url => {:action => "add_photo" },
        :accept => "photos",
        :droponempty => "true",
        :loading => visual_effect(:fade),
        :complete => visual_effect(:highlight, 'sortable_thumbs')
        ) %>
```

Just like the draggable_element helper, the drop_receiving_element helper expects the ID of the HTML element onto which you can drop something that was declared as draggable. The remaining parameters are options that given as name/value pairs (the order is not important). These options are doing a lot, so let's go through them one at a time:

:update => "slideshow-thumbs"
: This gives the ID of the HTML element that should be updated when a photo is dropped on our slideshow-contents div. The :position and :url options say how, and with what, that HTML element should be updated. When the :position option is omitted (as it is here), the HTML returned from the server *replaces* the target element's HTML. The :position option says that the returned HTML should be inserted into target element, instead of replacing it. The value :position can be specified as :before, :top, :bottom, and :after.

:url => {:action => "add_photo" }
: This option constructs the URL that is sent to the server (via a background Ajax request) when a photo is dropped (you've seen this before). This executes the add_photo method in the current controller (the SlideshowsController). The add_ photo action adds the dropped photo to the slideshow and returns an HTML fragment that will replace the existing HTML in the target element, which, as you will see, is a rerendering of the slideshow's contents, which now include the added photo.

:accept => "photos"
: Without this option, you could drop any draggable element here. However, this line says that only HTML elements that have the class attribute "photos" can be

dropped here. Remember that in our photo picker template we gave each photo class attribute of "photos".

`:droponempty => "true"`

This option says that the user can drop photos here even if the target is completely empty.

`:loading => visual_effect(:fade)`

`:complete => visual_effect(:highlight, 'sortable_thumbs')`

:loading and :complete (plus a few more events) specify client-side JavaScript event handlers that are executed at specific points in the progress of the Ajax request. In both cases, we are displaying a visual effect that gives the user positive feedback. The :loading event occurs when the browser begins loading the response, and the :complete event occurs when its all finished. The code specifies that the dropped photo will fade until it becomes invisible. It also highlights the target area on which the photo was dropped.

Now we need to create the add_photo method to actually add a dropped photo to the slideshow. Edit *photos/app/controllers/slideshows_controller.rb*, and add this:

```ruby
def add_photo
  slideshow_id = session[:slideshow].id
  photo_id = params[:id].split("_")[1]
  slide = Slide.new( )
  slide.photo_id = photo_id
  slide.slideshow_id = slideshow_id
  if !slide.save
    flash[:notice] = 'Error: unable to add photo.'
  end
  @slideshow = Slideshow.find(slideshow_id)
  session[:slideshow] = @slideshow
  render_partial 'show_slides_draggable'
end
```

Let's walk through this code:

`slideshow_id = session[:slideshow].id`

This line retrieves the current slideshow from the session hash and gets the slideshow's id.

`photo_id = params[:id].split("_")[1]`

The id attribute of the dropped photo get passed as the :id parameter. If you recall from the *photo_picker* template, we set those ids to values such as "photo_1" and "photo_19", so the remainder of this line of code splits the string on the underscore, grabs the second half, and assigns it to photo_id.

The next five lines create a new slide, assign to it the photo id and the slideshow id, and then save it to the database.

Finally, we render and return the show_slides_draggable partial, after setting @slideshow to the current slideshow (which is needed by the partial template).

All that code handles dragging new photos to add to the slideshow. Now we just need to add a little more code to implement dragging a photo from the slideshow to the unused photos list as an intuitive way to remove photos from the slideshow.

The displayed list of photos in the slideshow are already draggable because we made them into a sortable list. The only problem with the current implementation is that the photos can be dragged vertically only. They need to be dragged both vertically for reordering *and* horizontally to the unused photos column.

We can drag the photos only vertically because the default option for a sortable list is `:constraint => 'vertical'`. Fortunately, you can change this by editing the file *photos/app/views/slideshows/_show_slides_draggable.rhtml* and changing the call to the `sortable_element` helper to add this `:constraint` option:

```
<%= sortable_element('sortable_thumbs',
                     :url => {:action => 'update_slide_order'},
                     :constraint => '') %>
```

Now you can drag those photos anywhere. But you still need to make the unused photos list into a drop receiver that uses Ajax to remove the dropped photo from the slideshow.

To do so, edit *photos/app/views/slideshows/edit.rhtml,* and add this at the end:

```
<%= drop_receiving_element("slideshow-photo-picker",
        :update => "slideshow-photos",
        :url => {:action => "remove_slide" },
        :accept => "slides",
        :droponempty => "true",
        :loading => visual_effect(:fade),
        :complete => visual_effect(:highlight, 'slideshow-photos')
        ) %>
```

This code is almost identical to the other `drop_receiving_element` we used. The difference is that the target is the `slideshow-photo-picker`, and the action taken on a drop is to call the `remove_slide` method. Also, notice that you can drop only "slides" here (that is, HTML elements with a class attribute of `slides`). If you go back and take a look at how we defined the partial template *photos/app/views/slideshows/_show_slides_draggable.rhtml*, you will see that we did, indeed, make each item in the sortable list a slide.

Add the `remove_slide` method to *photos/app/controllers/slideshows_controller.rb*:

```
def remove_slide
  slideshow_id = session[:slideshow].id
  slide_id = params[:id].split("_")[1]
  Slide.delete(slide_id)
  @slideshow = Slideshow.find(slideshow_id)
  session[:slideshow] = @slideshow
  @photos = unused_photos(@slideshow)
  render_partial 'photo_picker'
end
```

In this code, you get the id of slide you want to remove, and then delete it from the slide database table. Remember, this action does not delete the photo from the database. The slide data says what photos are in a given slideshow, and deleting an entry from the slide table removes that slide from its slideshow. Finally, you render the HTML for the photo picker, which now includes the removed slide.

I'll bet you're anxious to see all this in action. All you need to do is to update the style sheet and then try it out. Edit *photos/public/stylesheets/slideshows.css*, and add the following:

```
#slideshow-photo-picker {
    float: left;
    width: 10em;
    text-align: center;
    border-right: thin solid #bbb;
    padding: 0.50em;
    padding-bottom: 10em;
}

img.thumbnail {
    border: 2px solid black;
    margin-bottom: 1em;
}

img.photos {
    border: 2px solid black;
    margin-bottom: 1em;
}
```

Whew! That's it: try it now!

The first thing you'll notice is that the Unused Photos section is empty (see Figure 6-5). That's because all the photos are currently in the slideshow. Just drag a few of the slides out of the slideshow and drop them into the Unused Photos column; then you'll have something more like Figure 6-6.

## Filtering by Category

Displaying all unused photos might seem acceptable right now, but we have only nine photos. If there were 900, it would quickly become unusable. So, our final feature in this chapter will be to display only the unused photos in a particular category.

The first thing to do in our controller is get a list of all categories that can populate the drop-down selection box. Edit *photos/app/controllers/slideshows_controller.rb*, and add this line to the end of the edit method:

```
@all_categories = Category.find(:all, :order=>"name")
```

This line retrieves a list of categories that can populate a drop-down selection box that the user will use to display only those unused photos that are in the selected category.

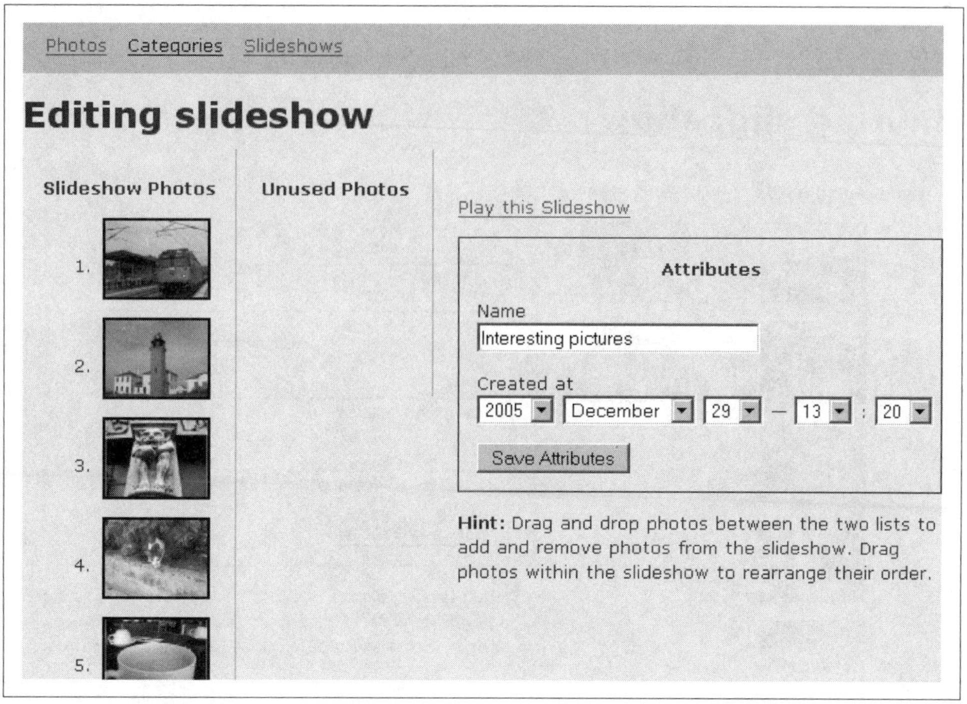

*Figure 6-5. Drag and drop add and remove*

Now, edit *photos/app/views/slideshows/edit.rhtml*, and add this right after the 'Play this Slideshow' line:

```
<p>
  <label for="category_id">Filter "Unused Photos" on this Category</label><br/>
  <%= collection_select(:category, :id, @all_categories, :id, :long_name) %>
  <%= observe_field(:category_id,
              :frequency => 2.0,
              :update => 'slideshow-photos',
              :url => { :action => 'change_filter'},
              :with => 'category_id' ) %>
</p>
```

The collection_select helper is normally used inside an HTML form, but here we are using it because it conveniently knows how to display a collection in a drop-down box. It will never be submitted as part of a form.

As shown, the observe_field helper checks the category drop-down box for changes every two seconds. When a change is detected, an Ajax request is fired off to the change_filter method, which returns new HTML (that has been appropriately filtered) to replace the slideshow-photos section.

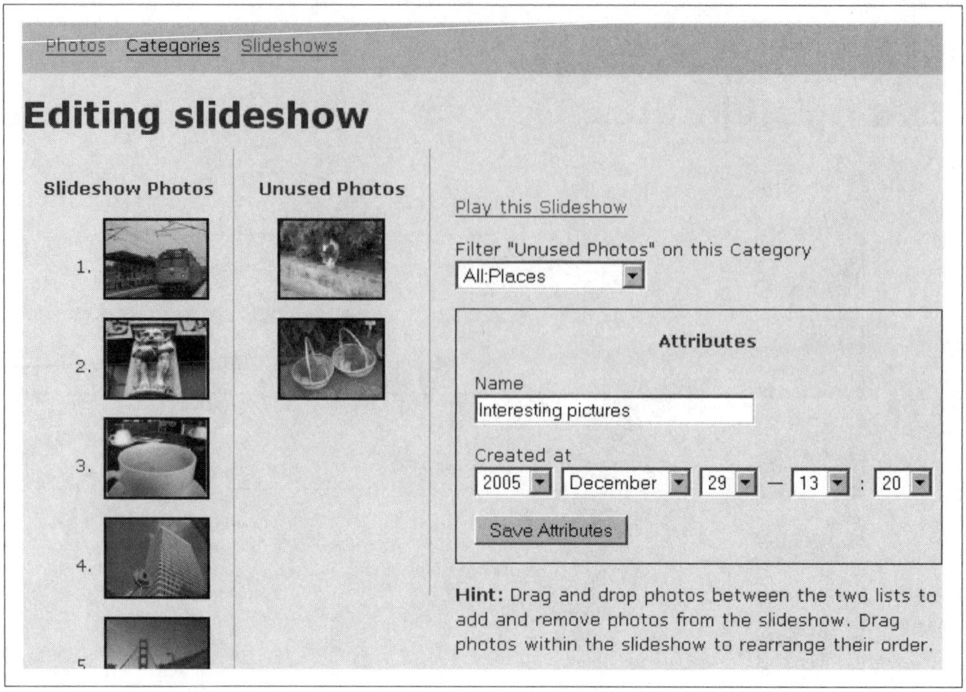

*Figure 6-6. Some unused photos*

The Category model class automatically shows a collection of all photos that are in a particular category. However, we need to get a collection of photos that are in a given category and in all of its child categories.

Edit *photos/app/models/category.rb*, and add this method:

```
def photos_including_child_categories
  result = photos.clone
  children.each do |c|
    c.photos_including_child_categories.each {|p|
      result << p if not result.include? p}
  end
  result
end
```

This method recursively collects a list of all photos in its own category and all of its child categories. You can use this in to get the list of unused photos to display.

In the meantime, edit *photos/app/controllers/slideshows_controller.rb* to add the change_filter method:

```
def change_filter
  slideshow_id = session[:slideshow].id
  category_id = params[:category_id] || 1
  session[:category_id] = category_id
  @slideshow = Slideshow.find(slideshow_id)
```

```
    session[:slideshow] = @slideshow
    @photos = unused_photos(@slideshow)
    render_partial 'photo_picker'
  end
```

This method stores the chosen category id in the session hash, retrieves a new list of unused photos, and then renders the photo_picker. Notice the bold code line in the previous code. This line tries to retrieve the category id from the request parameters. If there aren't any parameters, params[:category_id] returns nil, and the || operator returns the rightmost argument ("1" in this case).

Also, in this slideshow controller, we need to update the method that retrieves the unused photos to pay attention to the category setting. Do so by editing the unused_photos method; then replace the line all_photos = Photo.find(:all) with the following:

```
category_id = session[:category_id] || 1
session[:category_id] = category_id
category = Category.find(category_id)
all_photos = category.photos_including_child_categories
```

We're done; we've added category filtering! Fire up your browser, and try it (you may need to assign some categories to some unused photos). Now it looks like Figure 6-7.

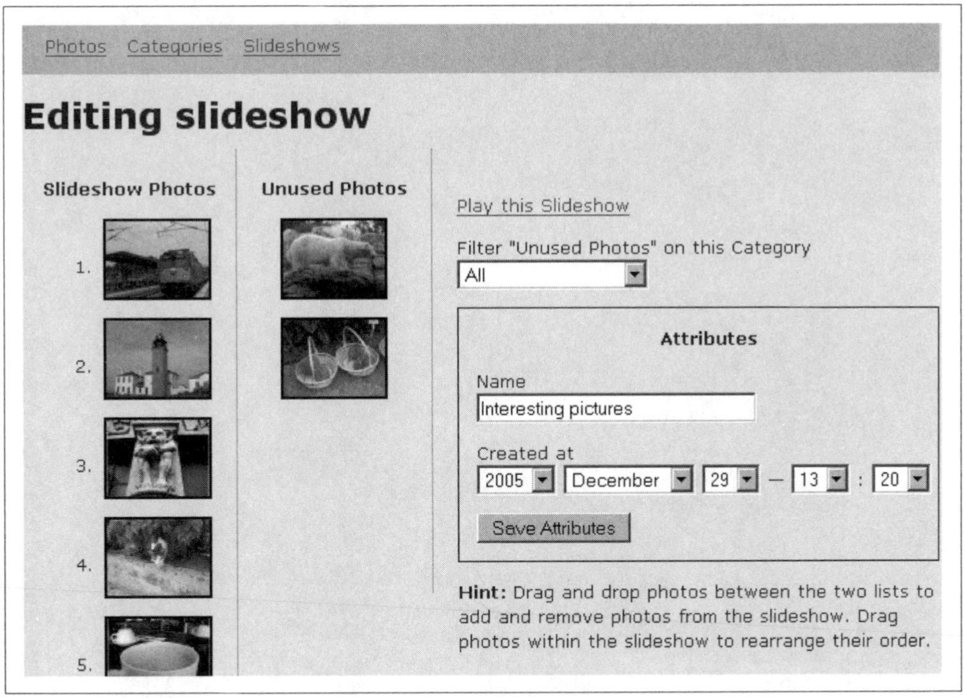

Figure 6-7. Filtering on categories

We've come a long way in a very short time. With fewer than 200 lines of code, we've added drag-and-drop capability to add and reorder slides. We've also added the core capability to actually show a slideshow. Ajax made our application much easier to use and more attractive. Next, we'll look into testing this application.

# CHAPTER 7

# Testing

You probably always write automated tests for all your software . . . or feel guilty for skipping them. Dynamically typed languages such as Ruby don't have a compile step that can catch errors, as Java or C++ does. Well, you'll be happy to know that Ruby on Rails makes automated testing very easy. In Rails, testing is not something that was bolted on afterwards. Testing has been built in from the very beginning. Rails was designed to be testable and to produce applications that are testable. It is so easy to create automated tests for a Rails application that you *should* feel guilty if you don't!

We've come this far with our Photo Share web application, but we haven't yet created any tests. In truth, this was deliberate. You had enough new things to learn as it was. But now it is time to rectify that oversight and start adding tests to our application. So let's skip the guilt and code some tests.

## Background

Instead of wasting time running through the litany of reasons why automated testing is probably the single most important thing you can do to increase the quality and reliability of your software, we'll get right down to it. If you haven't gotten the testing religion yet, just Google for "benefits automated testing."

Rails encourages you to create a well-tested application by actively generating default test cases and setting up scripts and tools to run three different kinds of tests. For example, when you use `script/generate` to create your models and controllers, Rails also generates skeleton test files for you to fill out with tests for your application. Rails also includes convenient console commands for running your tests.

Rails has a number of features that make it easy to test your application. In particular, Rails uses a separate runtime database dedicated to testing and can automatically populate the test database with fresh sample data (that you provide) before each test. Testing database-driven applications has always been a headache for developers, but Rails has managed to make it relatively painless.

# Ruby's Test::Unit

Ruby uses a testing framework known as Test::Unit (sometimes referred to as *test/unit*) to run your application's tests. Test::Unit is similar to the xUnit frameworks that you find in other programming languages, and implements four major concepts:

- An *assertion* is a single line of code that evaluates an expression and tests the results against an expected value. For example, you might assert that a password is at least six characters long; failing an assertion fails the associated test.

- A *test* is a method, whose name begins with test_, that contains a number of related assertions that, taken together, test one small piece of your application. For example, test_for_disallowed_passwords might contain assertions that verify that bad passwords are rejected (such as a password that is too short, contains all spaces, or is the word "password").

- A *test case* class is a subclass of Test::Unit::TestCase that contains a collection of test methods designed to test a functional area of your application. For our photo share application, we might have a test case class that tests everything having to do with categories.

- A *test suite* is a collection of test cases. When you run a test suite, it executes the tests in each test case that it contains. You won't need to use this with Rails applications, because Rails handles the task of running all your test cases.

Suppose you have the following non-Rails class:

```
class BasicNumber

  def initialize( number )
    @value = number
  end

  def add( x )
    @value + x
  end

  def multiply( x )
    @value * x
  end

end
```

Here is an example of a set of tests for this class:

```
require "basic_number.rb"
require "test/unit"

class TestBasicNumber < Test::Unit::TestCase

  def test_basic_add
    num = BasicNumber.new(16)
    assert_equal(20, num.add(4) )
```

```
      assert_equal(0, num.add(-16) )
      # this test will fail, to show what happens on failure
      assert_equal(100, num.add(99), "Adding 99 doesn't work")
    end

    def test_basic_multiply
      num = BasicNumber.new(16)
      assert_equal(32, num.multiply(2) )
      assert_equal(8, num.multiply(0.5) )
    end

  end
```

When you run this test file, it produces this output:

```
>ruby test_basic_number.rb
Loaded suite test_basic_number
Started
F.
Finished in 0.015 seconds.

  1) Failure:
test_basic_add(TestBasicNumber) [test_basic_number.rb:11]:
Adding 99 doesn't work.
<100> expected but was
<115>.

2 tests, 5 assertions, 1 failures, 0 errors
```

When you run the test class, it automatically runs all the tests. You don't need to explicitly call a test runner or create a test suite. Just subclassing Test::Unit:: TestCase and running the file causes the tests to be executed.

Test::Unit provides a large number of assertions you can use, and Table 7-1 shows the main ones. Most assert methods take an optional message parameter. If a message is included, then that message is displayed if its assertion fails.

*Table 7-1. Commonly used assertions*

| Assertion | Description |
|---|---|
| assert( boolean, [msg] ) | Passes if boolean is true |
| assert_equal( expected, actual, [msg] )<br>assert_not_equal( expected, actual, [msg] ) | Passes if expected == actual |
| assert_match( pattern, string, [msg] )<br>assert_no_match( pattern, string, [msg] ) | Passes if string =~ pattern |
| assert_nil( object, [msg] )<br>assert_not_nil( object, [msg] ) | Passes if object == nil |
| assert_instance_of( class, object, [msg] )<br>assert_kind_of( class, object, [msg] ) | Passes if object.class == class<br><br>Passes if object.kind_of?(class) |
| assert_raise( Exception, ... ) {block}<br>assert_nothing_raised( Exception, ...) {block} | Passes if the block raises (or doesn't) one of the listed exceptions |

You can define two special methods in your test case class: setup and teardown. Just before each test method is executed, setup is called to allow you to set up the environment for the test (open a database connection, load test data, and so on). Likewise, immediately after each test method returns, teardown is called to clean up and release any resources acquired by setup.

# Testing in Rails

Rails extends the Test::Unit framework to include new assertion methods that are specific to web applications and to the Ruby on Rails framework. Rails also provides explicit higher-level support for testing by including a consistent method for loading test data and a mechanism for running different types of test.

## Unit Tests, Functional Tests, and Integration Tests

In Rails, these three types of tests have very specific meanings that may differ from what you expect:

- Unit tests are for testing models.
- Functional tests are for testing controllers.
- Integration tests are for testing higher-level scenarios that exercise interactions between controllers.

Look at your Photo Share application's directory tree, and you'll find that it contains a *test* subdirectory. All tests reside under this *test* subdirectory, which has several subdirectories of its own:

*unit*
> Holds all unit tests.

*functional*
> Holds all functional tests.

*integration*
> Holds all integration tests.

*fixtures*
> Contains sample data for all tests (more on this later).

Take a look at *photos/test/unit*, and you'll see that it already contains *category_test.rb*, *photo_test.rb*, *slide_test.rb*, and *slideshow_test.rb*. These are test case skeletons created by Rails when we generated our model classes. But before you can start filling these skeleton test files, you first need to understand Rails' environments and fixtures.

### Environments

We software developers have always distinguished between code running in some form of development mode versus production mode. Development mode usually offers features such as active debugging, logging, and array bounds checking. These all add unnecessary overhead, so you should normally strip those conveniences out of your delivered production code.

This distinction of development versus production has usually been informal and ad hoc. As introduced in Chapter 2, Rails formalizes this practice using what it calls *environments*. Rails comes with three predefined environments: development, test, and production. You can also define new environments if you like, but most developers don't.

Each environment can have its own database and runtime settings. For example, in production mode, you usually want as much caching as possible to maximize performance, but in development mode, you want all caching disabled so that you can make a change and then immediately see it work. The predefined Rails environments have the default settings that make sense for each environment.

There are several ways to tell Rails what environment to use:

- Set the operating system environment variable `RAILS_ENV` to `'development'`, `'production'`, or `'test'`.
- Specify the environment value in *config/environment.rb* with a line of Ruby code like this: `ENV['RAILS_ENV'] = 'production'`.
- Use the –e option on the `script/server` script to start the WEBrick server. For example, `script/server –e production` starts the web server in production mode. Development mode is the default.

Take a look at the Photo Share application's *config/environments* directory and you will find three files: *development.rb*, *test.rb*, and *production.rb*. Each file contains the settings for its environment. These default environments are pretty well thought out, and it is unlikely that you will need to change them. But you should change the database settings for each environment. At the beginning of this book, we set up the development database, and now we need to set up the test database. Edit *config/database.yml*, and make sure that the test section looks like this:

```
test:
  adapter: mysql
  database: photos_test
  username: <your userid>
  password: <your password>
  socket: localhost
```

Start the *mysql* command prompt (`mysql –u <username> -p <password>`). Then, create a database called photos_test:

```
mysql> create database photos_test;
Query OK, 1 row affected (0.05 sec)
```

Now we can use a built-in feature of Rails to clone the database schema from the production database to the test database. Open a console window, navigate to the root directory of the Photo Share application, and run the command:

```
> rake db:test:clone_structure
```

You now have a test database that is identical to the development database, except that the tables do not contain any data. Getting data into these tables to use in our test is what fixtures are all about.

### Fixtures

*Fixtures* contain test data that Rails loads into your models before executing each test. You create your fixture data in the *test/fixtures* directory, and they can be in either CSV (comma-separated value) or YAML (YAML Ain't Markup Language) format.

YAML is the preferred format because it is so simple and readable, consisting mostly of keyword/value pairs. CSV files are useful when you have existing data in a database or spreadsheet that you can export to CSV format.

Fixtures for a particular database table should have the same filename as the database table name. So, to have fixtures for our photos database table, you would have a *photos.yml* file in the *test/fixtures* directory. Rails created a placeholder *photos.yml* when you created the photos model. Edit this existing *test/fixtures/photos.yml* file, and replace its contents with this:

```
train_photo:
  id: 1
  filename:     train.jpg
  created_at:   2006-04-01 03:20:49
  thumbnail:    t_train.jpg
  description:  This is a cool train!

lighthouse_photo:
  id: 2
  filename:     lighthouse.jpg
  created_at:   2006-04-02 14:58:49
  thumbnail:    t_lighthouse.jpg
  description:  My favorite lighthouse.
```

YAML is sensitive to whitespace, so be sure to use spaces instead of tabs, and eliminate any trailing spaces or tabs. These same two fixtures in CSV format look like this in a *photos.csv* file (in CSV format):

```
id, filename, created_at, thumbnail, description
1, train.jpg, "2006-04-01 03:20:49", t_train.jpg, "This is a cool train!"
2, lighthouse.jpg, "2006-04-02 14:58:49", t_lighthouse.jpg, "My favorite"
```

In the YAML file, the first line of each fixture is a name that is assigned to that fixture. (A little bit later, you will see how you can use this name.) The remaining lines are keyword/value pairs, one for each column in the database table.

Now that we have a test database and some fixtures, we can actually start writing some tests.

## Unit tests

In Rails, unit tests are for testing your models. The file *photos/test/unit/photo_test.rb*, for example, is where to create tests to test the Photo model. Rails created a skeleton of this file when we created the model. It currently looks like this:

```
require File.dirname(__FILE__) + '/../test_helper'

class PhotoTest < Test::Unit::TestCase
  fixtures :photos

  # Replace this with your real tests.
  def test_truth
    assert_kind_of Photo, photos(:first)
  end
end
```

Let's walk through the code a line at a time:

`require File.dirname(__FILE__) + '/../test_helper'`

There are some serious Ruby idioms in this line of code, but the net result is to instruct Ruby to require (load) the file *test_helper.rb* from the parent directory (*photos/test*). *test_helper.rb* activates the Rails environment so that our tests are ready to run. `__FILE__` is a special Ruby constant that contains the full path of the currently executing file. The `File.dirname` method takes that full path and removes the filename, returning only the directory path.

`class PhotoTest < Test::Unit::TestCase`

This code makes the `PhotoTest` class a subclass of `Test::Unit::TestCase`, as is required for running tests using `Test::Unit`.

`fixtures :photos`

This code tells Rails to load sample photo data into the database before each test (any existing data in the database is purged first). You can load multiple fixtures in one statement like this: `fixtures :photos, :categories, slideshows`.

It's finally time to create and run our first test. Edit *photos/test/unit/photo_test.rb*, and then add this code in the place of `test_truth`:

```
def test_photo_count
  assert_equal 3, Photo.count
end
```

This test is going to fail because it is asserting that the Photo database table contains three rows, but *photos.yml* contains only two. Lets try it and see. Open a command prompt, navigate to the root directory of our Photo Share application, and run this command:

```
> rake test:units
```

You should see the following output:

```
Started
.F..
Finished in 0.313 seconds.

  1) Failure:
test_photo_count(PhotoTest) [./test/unit/photo_test.rb:7]:
<3> expected but was
<2>.

4 tests, 4 assertions, 1 failures, 0 errors
```

Remember that the *test/units* directory contains four test files (even though we have modified only one of them), so this test ran all four. As expected, our test failed. Let's fix that:

```
def test_photo_count
  assert_equal 2, Photo.count
end
```

When you run the unit tests, you get:

```
Started
....
Finished in 0.359 seconds.

4 tests, 4 assertions, 0 failures, 0 errors
```

You know that fixtures are used to populate our database tables. But you can also individually access each fixture's data using the fixture's name.* photos(:train_photo).attributes returns a hash containing all the keyword/value pairs for the train_photo fixture, so photos(:train_photo).attributes['id'] returns the value of the id property (which is 1). More interestingly, you can retrieve an entire fixture's entry from the database using its name:

```
photo = photos(:train_photo)
```

Retrieving the train_photo object from the database by name is the equivalent to retrieving it by id:

```
photo = Photo.find(1)
```

Let's use this feature to add another test to *photos/test/unit/photo_test.rb*:

```
def test_photo_content
  assert_equal photos(:train_photo).attributes['id'], 1
  assert_equal photos(:train_photo), Photo.find(1)
  assert_equal photos(:lighthouse_photo).attributes['id'], 2
  assert_equal photos(:lighthouse_photo), Photo.find(2)
end
```

---

* Only the YAML format allows you to name a fixture, so if you use the CSV format, you will not be able to do this.

---

When you run the unit tests, you get:

```
Started
.....
Finished in 0.359 seconds.

5 tests, 8 assertions, 0 failures, 0 errors
```

Before we move on to functional tests, let's write one more test that exercises our ability to perform basic CRUD operations with our Photo model. Once again, edit *photos/test/unit/photo_test.rb*, and add:

```ruby
def test_photo_crud
  # create a new photo
  cat = Photo.new
  cat.filename = 'cat.jpg'
  cat.created_at = DateTime.now
  cat.thumbnail = 't_cat.jpg'
  cat.description = 'This is my cat!'

  # save it to the database
  assert cat.save

  # read it back from the database
  assert_not_nil cat2 = Photo.find(cat.id)

  # make sure they are the same
  assert_equal cat, cat2

  # modify this cat and update the database
  cat2.description = 'A ghost of my cat.'
  assert cat2.save

  # delete it from the database
  assert cat2.destroy
end
```

Let's run the test again and see whether this is going to pass:

```
Started
......
Finished in 0.594 seconds.

6 tests, 13 assertions, 0 failures, 0 errors
```

With our guilt suitably assuaged, let's move on to functional tests.

## Functional tests

In Rails, you'll use functional tests to exercise one feature, or function, in your controllers. Functional and integration tests check the responses to web commands, called *HTTP requests*. In this section, we work on functional tests for the photos controller.

We originally created our photos controller by generating scaffolding for it. When you generate scaffolding for a database table, Rails creates a remarkably complete set of functional tests:

```
require File.dirname(__FILE__) + '/../test_helper'
require 'photos_controller'

# Reraise errors caught by the controller.
class PhotosController; def rescue_action(e) raise e end; end

class PhotosControllerTest < Test::Unit::TestCase
  fixtures :photos

  def setup
    @controller = PhotosController.new
    @request    = ActionController::TestRequest.new
    @response   = ActionController::TestResponse.new
  end

  def test_index
    get :index
    assert_response :success
    assert_template 'list'
  end

  def test_list
    get :list

    assert_response :success
    assert_template 'list'

    assert_not_nil assigns(:photos)
  end

  def test_show
    get :show, :id => 1

    assert_response :success
    assert_template 'show'

    assert_not_nil assigns(:photo)
    assert assigns(:photo).valid?
  end

  def test_new
    get :new

    assert_response :success
    assert_template 'new'

    assert_not_nil assigns(:photo)
  end
```

```ruby
  def test_create
    num_photos = Photo.count

    post :create, :photo => {}

    assert_response :redirect
    assert_redirected_to :action => 'list'

    assert_equal num_photos + 1, Photo.count
  end

  def test_edit
    get :edit, :id => 1

    assert_response :success
    assert_template 'edit'

    assert_not_nil assigns(:photo)
    assert assigns(:photo).valid?
  end

  def test_update
    post :update, :id => 1
    assert_response :redirect
    assert_redirected_to :action => 'show', :id => 1
  end

  def test_destroy
    assert_not_nil Photo.find(1)

    post :destroy, :id => 1
    assert_response :redirect
    assert_redirected_to :action => 'list'

    assert_raise(ActiveRecord::RecordNotFound) {
      Photo.find(1)
    }
  end
end
```

These tests are in the file *photos/test/functional/photos_controller_test.rb* and cover the full range of CRUD operations. The Rails-generated functional tests for our other controllers are very similar.

You can run the functional tests with the command rake test:functionals but be forewarned that you will see a lot of errors! You might think that our Photo Share application has many problems, but the problem is that our tests are simply out of date. Those tests worked perfectly fine when they were first created and we were using the scaffolding for everything. But since that time, we have made lots of changes to the code yet never changed the tests to keep up with the evolving code base. Now we need to fix these tests.

For the purposes of this chapter, we are going to get the photo controller's functional tests working to give you enough understanding to fix the others yourself. To simplify the test reports, move all functional tests in *photos/test/functional*, except for *photos_controller_test.rb*, to another directory for safe keeping.

Because you can assign every photo to one or more categories, a lot of the photo controller code also works with categories. But we don't yet have any test categories, only test photos. So the first thing to do is to create some fixtures for the *categories* table and the *categories_photos* join table.

Edit the file *photos/test/fixtures/categories.yml*, and replace its contents with this:

```
all:
  id: 1
  name: All

people:
  id: 2
  name: People
  parent_id: 1

animals:
  id: 3
  name: Animals
  parent_id: 1

things:
  id: 4
  name: Things
  parent_id: 1
```

Now create the file *photos/test/fixtures/categories_photos.yml* with this content:

```
train_category:
  photo_id: 1
  category_id: 4

lighthouse_category:
  photo_id: 2
  category_id: 4
```

Finally, edit *photos/test/functional/photos_controller_test.rb,* and add these two lines at the beginning of the class definition for `CategoriesControllerTest`:

```
fixtures :categories
fixtures :categories_photos
```

Let's try running our functional tests. From the base directory of our Photo Share application, run this command:

```
> rake test:functionals
Started
F.......
Finished in 0.469 seconds.
```

```
1) Failure:
test_create(PhotosControllerTest) [./test/functional/photos_controller_test.rb:5
5]:
Expected response to be a <:redirect>, but was <200>

8 tests, 25 assertions, 1 failures, 0 errors
```

Hmmm: that wasn't exactly error-free; there was an assertion failure in the method test_create:

```
def test_create
  num_photos = Photo.count

  post :create, :photo => { }

  assert_response :redirect
  assert_redirected_to :action => 'list'

  assert_equal num_photos + 1, Photo.count
end
```

This test tries to create a new photo by posting a request to the create action of the current controller (which is the photo controller). We expected that the create action would save a new photo to the database and then redirect to the list action. Instead, we got an *http 200* response (which is a normal, everything's OK, response).

A quick look at the create method shows that if the save to the database fails, then the controller renders and returns the new template, which correctly returns an *http 200* response:

```
def create
  @photo = Photo.new(params[:photo])
  @photo.categories = Category.find(params[:categories]) if params[:categories]
  if @photo.save
    flash[:notice] = 'Photo was successfully created.'
    redirect_to :action => 'list'
  else
    @all_categories = Category.find(:all, :order=>"name")
    render :action => 'new'
  end
end
```

Why would the save to the database (@photo.save) fail? Let's take a look at the photo model (*photos/app/models/photo.rb*) to see whether that gives us any idea:

```
class Photo < ActiveRecord::Base
  has_many :slides
  has_and_belongs_to_many :categories
  validates_presence_of :filename
end
```

If you look closely, you'll see the culprit within the validation: validates_presence_of :filename. This code will refuse to save any instance of Photo to the database if it does not contain a filename; our test did not assign a filename. To fix that problem, edit *photos/test/functional/photos_controller_test.rb* to look like this:

```
def test_create
  num_photos = Photo.count

  post :create, :photo => {:filename => 'myphoto.jpg'}

  assert_response :redirect
  assert_redirected_to :action => 'list'

  assert_equal num_photos + 1, Photo.count
end
```

When you run the functional tests again, you'll see:

```
> rake test:functionals
Started
........
Finished in 0.468 seconds.

8 tests, 28 assertions, 0 failures, 0 errors
```

Excellent. All the functional tests for the photos controller are now succeeding.

Did you notice that functional tests for the photos controller use a lot of assertions that are not part of Test::Unit but seem to be specific to web development (assert_redirected_to) and even specific to Rails (assert_template)? Rails provides these additional assertions. Table 7-2 shows all of the extra assertions provided by Rails.

*Table 7-2. Rails-supplied assertions*

| Assertion | Description |
| --- | --- |
| assert_dom_equal<br>assert_dom_not_equal | Asserts that two HTML strings are logically equivalent. |
| assert_generates | Asserts that the provided options can generate the provided path. |
| assert_tag | Asserts that there is a tag/node/element in the body of the response that meets all the given conditions. |
| assert_recognizes | Asserts that the routing rules successfully parse the given URL path. |
| assert_redirected_to | Asserts that the response is a redirect to the specified destination. |
| assert_response | Asserts that the response was the given HTTP status code (or range of status codes). |
| assert_routing | Asserts that path (URL) and options match both ways. |
| assert_template | Asserts that the request was rendered with the specified template file. |
| assert_valid | Asserts that the provided record is valid by active record standards. |

### Integration tests

Integration tests are a new feature in Rails 1.1. Integration tests are higher-level scenario tests that verify the interactions between the application's actions, across all controllers.

As you might have guessed by now, integration tests live in the *test/integration* directory and are run using the command rake test:integration.

Our Photo Share application hasn't yet been developed to the point where integration tests would be useful. Here, instead, is a hypothetical integration test to give you a feel for what they are like:

```
require "#{File.dirname(__FILE__)}/../test_helper"

class UserManagementTest < ActionController::IntegrationTest
  fixtures :users, :preferences

  def test_register_new_user
    get "/login"
    assert_response :success
    assert_template "login/index"

    get "/register"
    assert_response :success
    assert_template "register/index"

    post "/register",
         :user_name => "happyjoe",
         :password => "neversad"
    assert_response :redirect
    follow_redirect!
    assert_response :success
    assert_template "welcome"
  end
end
```

This test leads its application through the series of web pages that a new user would go through to register with the site. You can see that the scenario being tested is pretty easy to follow:

1. Send an HTTP GET request for the */login* page. Now check to see whether the request was successful and whether the response was rendered by the expected template.

2. Simulate the user clicking on the "register" button or link by sending an HTTP GET request for the */register* page. Again, check for the proper response.

3. Simulate the new user filling out and submitting the registration form by sending an HTTP POST request that includes user_name and password field values. Now verify that the response is a redirect, follow the redirect, and verify that you successfully end up on the welcome page.

Integration tests can be used to duplicate bugs that have been reported. Then, when you fix the bug, you will know it because your test will start succeeding. Plus, you then have a test in place that will alert you if the same bug ever reappears.

## Advanced Testing

Rails provides an impressive level of support for testing. But just in case that's not enough for you, here are a couple of third-party testing tools that are really on the cutting edge and worthy of your attention.

### ZenTest

Self-described as "testing on steroids," ZenTest provides a set of integrated testing tools to automate and streamline your testing. For example, *autotest* monitors your projects files for changes. When *autotest* detects a change, it automatically runs the appropriate test to verify that the change has not broken anything.

You can learn more about ZenTest at *http://www.zenspider.com/ZSS/Products/ZenTest/*.

### Selenium

Selenium is a testing tool written specifically for web applications. Selenium tests run directly in a browser, just as real applications do, provided it's a modern browser that supports JavaScript. As such, it is an ideal tool for testing the Ajax features of a web application.

You can learn more about Selenium on its home page at *http://www.openqa.org/selenium/*. IBM's developerWorks has a good article on using Selenium with Ruby on Rails at the following address: *http://www-128.ibm.com/developerworks/java/library/wa-selenium-ajax/index.html*.

# Wrapping Up

Testing concludes our whirlwind tour through the Rails framework. We've barely scratched the surface. Photo Share is not nearly complete. We could have easily added:

- Security, with the Rails login generator or one of the other login products. With a security model, you can let each user manage and share her own set of photos, instead of having one community model.
- Uploading photos. You need to let the user upload photos with some other means, but Rails provides excellent support for simple tasks such as file uploads.
- Deployment. We've not even touched on pushing the Photo Share application into production, but good tools such as Capistrano (*http://manuals.rubyonrails.com/read/book/17*) allow one-click deployment and also one-click reversal of changes.
- Comments and blogging. You can allow discussion about slides and slideshows. Simple support isn't difficult, but you can also build in the Typo blogging engine.

We've decided that these changes are beyond the scope of a quick-start book, but this list provides a sample of the community that's rapidly developing behind Rails. After this pass through Photo Share, you doubtlessly will be excited about doing more. In the appendixes that follow, we'll give you another whirlwind tour of what's available and how to find more information.

In Rails, an idea is rapidly crystallizing before our eyes as a real force in this industry, but this phenomenon is unlike anything you've ever seen before. So far, this explosion is happening within the open source community, without major commercial investment, and with an amazing amount of contribution from increasingly diverse contributors. The growth is fueled by a core of smart developers who understand that beautiful software can also be powerful, that useful development environments don't need to come from a corporation, and that real innovation doesn't always take the path you expect. We hope you've experienced a taste of what is to come. The rules are all changing. Welcome to the new game.

# Installing Rails

Ruby on Rails makes developing web applications easier and more productive than ever before. Not surprisingly, getting a Ruby on Rails development environment installed is pretty easy as well.

This appendix will show you how to get a Rails development environment installed. But be forewarned: this is a very short appendix because getting started is pretty darn easy.

## Windows

We present two options for a Windows installation of Ruby on Rails: Instant Rails and RadRails alone and Instant Rails plus the Rad Rails IDE.

### Instant Rails

The easiest way to get started on Windows is to use Instant Rails. Instant Rails (Figure A-1) is a one-stop Rails runtime solution containing Ruby, Rails, Apache, and MySQL, all preconfigured and ready to run. There is no installer, you simply unzip it into the directory of your choice and run it. It does not modify your system environment.

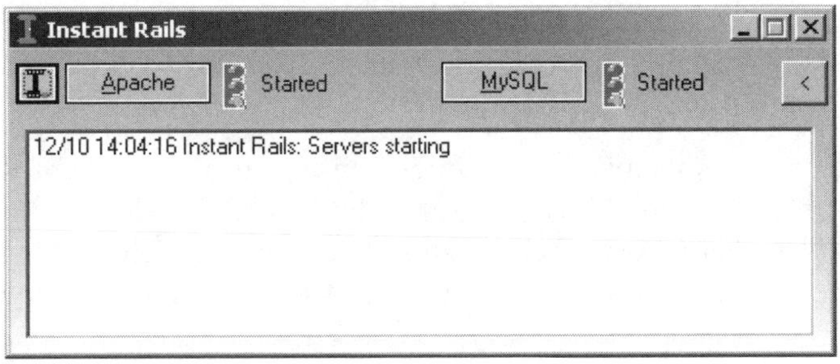

*Figure A-1. Instant Rails*

For more details about Instant Rails, go to the Instant Rails home page at *http://instantrails.rubyforge.org*:

1. Download and unzip the latest version of the Instant Rails ZIP file from: *http://rubyforge.org/frs/?group_id=904*.

2. Make sure that the installation path (to the directory into which you unzip the archive) does not contain any space characters, and then start *InstantRails.exe*.

3. Instant Rails will detect that it is being started from a new directory and ask whether you want to have it update the paths in the all of the configuration files. Click Yes.

4. Click on the "I" button (or press the Alt key twice) to display the main menu.

That's all there is to it!

Instant Rails includes the cookbook Rails application from the ONLamp.com article "Rolling with Ruby on Rails" (*http://www.onlamp.com/pub/a/onlamp/2005/01/20/rails.html*). The cookbook application is included as a preinstalled sample application. There is also a version of this tutorial that was rewritten to be specific to Instant Rails available at *http://instantrails.rubyforge.org/wiki/wiki.pl?Rolling_With_Ruby_On_Instant_Rails_Tutorial*. Instant Rails also includes the Photo Share application from this book.

Instant Rails includes the Apache web server, which you won't use until later in the development of a Rails application, when you want to more closely duplicate your final deployment environment. During development, it is easiest use Ruby's built-in web server, WEBrick, or the new Ruby Mongrel server.

So, for example, to run the cookbook application, execute the Instant Rails menu command Rails Applications → Manage Rails Applications..., select the checkbox next to the cookbook application, and press the "Start with WEBrick" button. When you browse to *http://127.0.0.1:3000/*, you will see the cookbook application.

Instant Rails includes the One-Click Ruby Installer for Windows for its Ruby interpreter, which includes the SciTE text editor with full Ruby syntax highlighting. After installing Instant Rails, you can find the SciTE executable at *InstantRails/ruby/scite/SciTE.exe*.

## RadRails

If you want more than a simple text editor, then try out the excellent RadRails IDE. RadRails (Figure A-2) is an Eclipse plug-in and is available as both a standalone IDE (Eclipse with the plug-in preinstalled) and as a standard Eclipse plug-in at *http://www.radrails.org*. With RadRails, you get a full IDE, complete with an integrated GUI debugger.

*Figure A-2. RadRails*

After you install RadRails, you have to configure it to work with your Instant Rails installation:

1. Execute the menu command Window → Preferences.

2. Select Ruby → Installed Interpreters.

3. Click the Add button, and give the new interpreter instance a name (like "Instant Rails Ruby"); browse to the Ruby executable at *InstantRails/ruby/bin/ruby.exe*, and click OK.

4. While still in the preferences dialog, select Ruby->Ri/rdoc and set the Rdoc and Ri paths to *InstantRails/ruby/bin/rdoc* and *InstantRails/ruby/bin/ri*, respectively. This step lets you use the built-in documentation features of RadRails.

You can create a new skeleton Rails application via the menus with File → New... → Rails → RailsProject.

# OS X

The easiest way to get started on OS X is to use Locomotive (Figure A-3), which is very similar to Instant Rails on Windows, except that it uses the Lighttpd for the web server (instead of Apache) and SQLite for the database (instead of MySQL). For more details about Locomotive, go to its home page at *http://locomotive.raaum.org*.

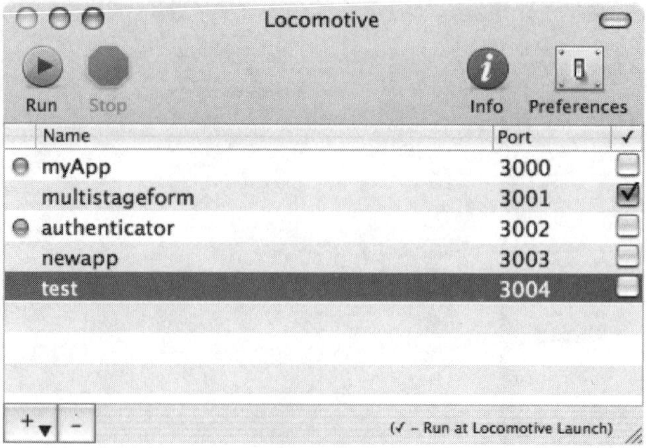

*Figure A-3. Locomotive*

1. Download Locomotive from *http://sourceforge.net/project/showfiles.php?group_id=146941* (you can also download the "Bundle" version that contains extra libraries, like Rmagick).

2. Simply drag and drop the file you just downloaded to your *Applications* folder.

3. This book uses MySQL for the development database, so we recommend that you install and use MySQL instead of the SQLite included in Locomotive. Download the latest MySQL packages from *http://dev.mysql.com/downloads/* and run the installer.

4. To start Locomotive, double-click *Locomotive.app*.

That's all there is to it!

## TextMate and RadRails

The commercial text-editor-on-steroids TextMate (Figure A-4) is very popular with Rails developers on OS X. Locomotive provides some minimal built-in support for TextMate. You can right-click a Rails app in Locomotive and choose to open its directory in TextMate.

TextMate is inexpensive, but not free. You can find out more about TextMate here: *http://macromates.com*.

If you want more than a pumped-up text editor, you'll be happy to know that the excellent RadRails IDE also runs on OS X. See the section "RadRails," earlier in this chapter.

Once installed, you can configure RadRails to work with your Locomotive installation by following the same steps shown in the Windows section of this appendix.

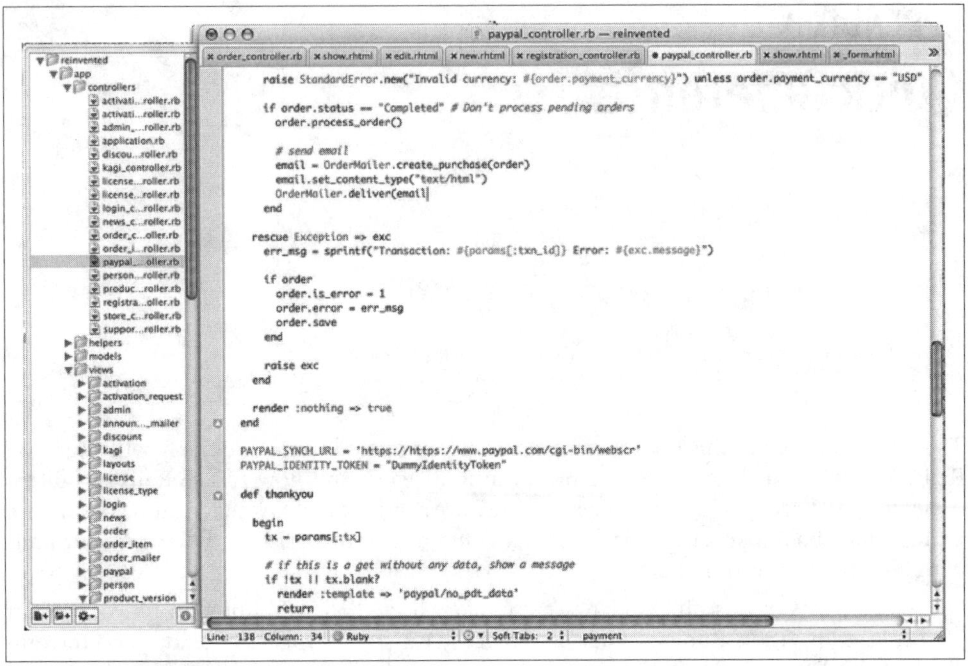

Figure A-4. TextMate

# Linux

There is no one simple way to install a Ruby on Rails development environment on a Linux distributions. Although the steps may be similar for each distribution, they are different enough that we will just point you to some external instructions. If you don't find your distribution here, try a Google search for "installing ruby on rails on <your-distro-here>".

Fedora Core
>    http://www.digitalmediaminute.com/howto/fc4rails/

Debian
>    http://www.debian-administration.org/articles/329

Gentoo
>    http://gentoo-wiki.com/HOWTO_RoR

Ubuntu (Hoary)
>    http://paulgoscicki.com/archives/2005/09/ruby-on-rails-on-ubuntu/

Ubuntu (Hoary) using XAMPP
>    http://townx.org/ruby_on_rails_on_xampp_with_fastcgi_for_ubuntu_hoary

SUSE
>    http://wiki.rubyonrails.org/rails/pages/RailsOnSUSE

# Quick Reference

The whole purpose of this book has been to get you up and running quickly with Ruby on Rails. You've learned how the core pieces of Rails work and how to use Rails to build a basic web application. Rails contains more features and capabilities than can be covered in a quick-start book like this. This appendix contains a concise list of the features of Rails with links to more information.

Substantial parts of this quick reference are taken from "What Is Ruby on Rails" by Curt Hibbs, * the "InVisible Ruby On Rails Reference 1.1.2" by InVisible GmbHd, † and the official Ruby on Rails API documentation (*http://api.rubyonrails.com*). This appendix is released under the Creative Commons license (*http://creativecommons.org/licenses/by-sa/2.5/*) and can be downloaded from this book's web site: *http://www.oreilly.com/catalog/rubyrails*.

## General

### Documentation

API for local installation
**gem_server**
*http:// localhost:8088/*

Official Rails API
*http://api.rubyonrails.com*

Searchable Rails API
*http://rails.outertrack.com*
*http://railshelp.com*

Ruby documentation
*http://ruby-doc.org*

---

* "What Is Ruby on Rails" was published at ONLamp.com in October 2005 (*http://www.onlamp.com/pub/a/onlamp/2005/10/13/what_is_rails.html*).

† The "InVisible Ruby On Rails Reference 1.1.2" was released under the Creative Commons license. The original version can be found at *http://blog.invisible.ch/files/rails-reference-1.1.html*.

Excellent multi-API documentation
  Includes Ruby, Ruby on Rails, HTML, CSS, JavaScript, DOM, and more: *http://www.gotapi.com*

## Supported Web Servers

  WEBrick
  Mongrel
  Lighttpd
  Apache
  MS IIS

Learn more: *http://wiki.rubyonrails.org/rails/pages/FAQ#webservers*.

## Supported Databases

  DB2
  Firebird
  MySQL
  Oracle
  PostgreSQL
  SQLite
  SQL Server

Learn more: *http://wiki.rubyonrails.org/rails/pages/DatabaseDrivers*.

## Integrated Development Environments (IDEs)

### Open Source

Eclipse/RDT
  *http://rubyeclipse.sourceforge.net*
FreeRIDE
  *http://freeride.rubyforge.org*
RadRails (built on Eclipse/RDT)
  *http://www.radrails.org*
RDE (Ruby Development Environment)
  *http://homepage2.nifty.com/sakazuki/rde_e.html*

### Commercial

ArachnoRuby
  *http://www.ruby-ide.com/ruby/ruby_ide_and_ruby_editor.php*
Komodo
  *http://www.activestate.com/Products/Komodo*

### Editors

Several options
  *http://wiki.rubyonrails.org/rails/pages/Editors*

### Debugging

Logfiles
> Look for the files *development.log*, *test.log*, and *production.log*.

Interactive Rails Console
> *http://wiki.rubyonrails.com/rails/pages/Console*
>
> *http://www.clarkware.com/cgi/blosxom/2006/04/04*

Breakpoint
> *http://wiki.rubyonrails.com/rails/pages/HowtoDebugWithBreakpoint*

Debuggers
> See the IDEs listed earlier.

Rails debug popup
> *http://www.bigbold.com/snippets/posts/show/697*

### Create a New Rails Application

```
rails app_name
```

Options:

**-d=*xxx*** *or* **--database=*xxx***
> Specify which database to use (mysql, oracle, postgresql, sqlite3, etc.); defaults to mysql.

**-r=*xxx*** *or* **--ruby-path=*xxx***
> Specify the path to Ruby; if not set, the scripts use env to find Ruby.

**-f** *or* **–freeze**
> Freezes Rails into the *vendor/rails* directory.

---

## Testing

```
rake test              # Test all units and functionals
rake test:functionals  # Run tests for functionals
rake test:integration  # Run tests for integration
rake test:units        # Run tests for units
```

### Unit Tests

```
rake test:units
```

Available assertions:

```
assert_kind_of Class, @var  # same class
assert @var                 # not nil
assert_equal 1, @p.id       # equality
@product.destroy
assert_raise(ActiveRecord::RecordNotFound) { Product.find( @product.id ) }
```

### Functional Tests

```
rake test:functionals
```

### Requests

```
get :action # a get request of the specificed action
get :action, :id => 1,
          { session_hash }, # optional session variables
          { flash_hash }    # optional messages in the flash

post :action, :foo => { :value1 => 'abc', :value2 => '123' },
             { :user_id => 17 },
             { :message => 'success' }

get, post, put, delete, head

assert_response :success
# possible parameters are:
#    :success
#    :redirect
#    :missing
#    :error
```

### Redirects

```
assert_redirected_to :action => :other_action
assert_redirected_to :controller => 'foo', :action => 'bar'
assert_redirected_to http://www.invisible.ch
```

### Rendered with Template

```
assert_template "post/index"
```

### Variable Assignments

```
assert_nil assigns(:some_variable)
assert_not_nil assigns(:some_variable)
assert_equal 17, assigns(:posts).size
```

### Rendering of Specific Tags

```
assert_tag :tag => 'body'
assert_tag :content => 'Rails Seminar'
assert_tag :tag => 'div', :attributes => { :class => 'index_list' }
assert_tag :tag => 'head', :parent => { :tag => 'body' }
assert_tag :tag => 'html', :child => { :tag => 'head' }
assert_tag :tag => 'body', :descendant => { :tag => 'div' }
assert_tag :tag => 'ul',
          :children => { :count => 1..3,
                         :only => { :tag => 'li' } }
```

## Integration Tests

```
rake test:integration
```

Hypothetical integration test:

```
require "#{File.dirname(__FILE__)}/../test_helper"

class UserManagementTest < ActionController::IntegrationTest
  fixtures :users, :preferences
```

```
def test_register_new_user
  get "/login"
  assert_response :success
  assert_template "login/index"

  get "/register"
  assert_response :success
  assert_template "register/index"

  post "/register",
       :user_name => "happyjoe",
       :password => "neversad"
  assert_response :redirect
  follow_redirect!
  assert_response :success
  assert_template "welcome"
end
```

Learn more: *http://jamis.jamisbuck.org/articles/2006/03/09/integration-testing-in-rails-1-1*.

## More on Testing

Learn more: *http://manuals.rubyonrails.com/read/book/5*.

## rake

rake is the Ruby version of a make utility. Rails defines a number of rake tasks:

```
rake db:fixtures:load          # Load fixtures into the current environment's
                               # database
                               # Load specific fixtures using FIXTURES=x,y
rake db:migrate                # Migrate the database through scripts in
                               # db/migrate. Target
                               # specific version with VERSION=x
rake db:schema:dump            # Create a db/schema.rb file that can be portably
                               # used against any DB supported by AR
rake db:schema:load            # Load a schema.rb file into the database
rake db:sessions:clear         # Clear the sessions table
rake db:sessions:create        # Creates a sessions table for use with
                               # CGI::Session::ActiveRecordStore
rake db:structure:dump         # Dump the database structure to a SQL file
rake db:test:clone             # Recreate the test database from the current
                               # environment's database schema
rake db:test:clone_structure   # Recreate the test databases from the development
                               # structure
rake db:test:prepare           # Prepare the test database and load the schema
rake db:test:purge             # Empty the test database

rake doc:app                   # Build the app HTML Files
rake doc:clobber_app           # Remove rdoc products
rake doc:clobber_plugins       # Remove plugin documentation
rake doc:clobber_rails         # Remove rdoc products
rake doc:plugins               # Generate documaion for all installed plugins
rake doc:rails                 # Build the rails HTML Files
rake doc:reapp                 # Force a rebuild of the RDOC files
```

```
rake doc:rerails              # Force a rebuild of the RDOC files

rake log:clear                # Truncates all *.log files in log/ to zero bytes

rake rails:freeze:edge        # Lock this application to latest Edge Rails. Lock a
                              # specific revision with REVISION=X
rake rails:freeze:gems        # Lock this application to the current gems (by
                              # unpacking them into vendor/rails)
rake rails:unfreeze           # Unlock this application from freeze of gems or
                              # edge and return to a fluid use of system gems

rake rails:update             # Update both scripts and public/javascripts from
                              # Rails
rake rails:update:javascripts # Update your javascripts from your current rails
                              # install
rake rails:update:scripts     # Add new scripts to the application script/
                              # directory

rake stats                    # Report code statistics (KLOCs, etc) from the
                              # application

rake test                     # Test all units and functionals
rake test:functionals         # Run tests for functionalsdb:test:prepare
rake test:integration         # Run tests for integrationdb:test:prepare
rake test:plugins             # Run tests for pluginsenvironment
rake test:recent              # Run tests for recentdb:test:prepare
rake test:uncommitted         # Run tests for uncommitteddb:test:prepare
rake test:units               # Run tests for unitsdb:test:prepare

rake tmp:cache:clear          # Clears all files and directories in tmp/cache
rake tmp:clear                # Clear session, cache, and socket files from tmp/
rake tmp:create               # Creates tmp directories for sessions, cache, and
                              # sockets
rake tmp:sessions:clear       # Clears all files in tmp/sessions
rake tmp:sockets:clear        # Clears all ruby_sess.* files in tmp/sessions
```

## Scripts

```
script/about               # Information about environenment
script/breakpointer        # starts the breakpoint server
script/console             # interactive Rails Console
script/destroy             # deletes files created by generators
script/generate            # -> generators
script/plugin              # -> Plugins
script/runner              # executes a task in the rails context
script/server              # launches the development server
                           # http://localhost:3000

script/performance/profiler     # profile an exspesive method
script/performance/benchmarker  # benchmark different methods

script/process/reaper
script/process/spawner
```

## Generators

```
ruby script/generate model ModellName
ruby script/generate controller ListController show edit
ruby script/generate scaffold ModelName ControllerName
ruby script/generate migration AddNewTable
ruby script/generate plugin PluginName
ruby script/generate mailer Notification lost_password signup
ruby script/generate web_service ServiceName api_one api_two
ruby script/generate integration_test TestName
ruby script/generate session_migration
```

Options:

-p *or* --pretend
> Run but do not make any changes.

-f *or* --force
> Overwrite files that already exist.

-s *or* --skip
> Skip files that already exist.

-q *or* --quiet
> Suppress normal output.

-t *or* --backtrace
> Debugging: show backtrace on errors.

-h *or* --help
> Show this help message.

-c *or* --svn
> Modify files with subversion (note: svn must be in path).

## Plug-ins

```
script/plugin discover            # discover plugin repositories
script/plugin list                # list all available plugins
script/plugin install where       # install the "where" plugin
script/plugin install -x where    # install where plugin as SVN external
script/plugin install http://invisible.ch/projects/plugins/where
script/plugin update              # update installed plugins
script/plugin source              # add a source repository
script/plugin unsource            # removes a source repository
script/plugin sources             # lists source repositories
```

Learn more: *http://wiki.rubyonrails.com/rails/pages/Plugins*.

Searchable directory of plug-ins: *http://www.agilewebdevelopment.com/plugins*.

---

## RJS (Ruby JavaScript)

This example:

```
update_page do |page|
  page.insert_html :bottom, 'list', "<li>#{@item.name}</li>"
  page.visual_effect :highlight, 'list'
  page.hide 'status-indicator', 'cancel-link'
end
```

---

generates the following JavaScript:

```
new Insertion.Bottom("list", "<li>Some item</li>");
new Effect.Highlight("list");
["status-indicator", "cancel-link"].each(Element.hide);
```

Learn more:

- *http://api.rubyonrails.com/classes/ActionView/Helpers/PrototypeHelper/ JavaScriptGenerator/GeneratorMethods.html*
- *http://www.codyfauser.com/articles/2005/11/20/rails-rjs-templates*
- *http://scottraymond.net/articles/2005/12/01/real-world-rails-rjs-templates*
- *http://www.rubynoob.com/articles/2006/05/13/simple-rails-rjs-tutorial*

# Active Record

## Automated Mapping

Automatically maps:

- Tables → classes
- Rows → objects (instances of model classes)
- Columns → object attributes

Table to class mapping uses English plurals:

- An Invoice model class maps to an invoices table.
- A Person model class maps to a people table.
- A Country model class maps to a countries table.
- A SecurityLevel model class maps to a security_levels table.

Learn more: *http://api.rubyonrails.com/classes/ActiveRecord/Base.html*.

## Associations

Four ways of associating models (Figures B-1 and B-2):

```
has_one
has_many
belongs_to
has_and_belongs_to_many
def Order < ActiveRecord::Base
  has_many :line_items
  belongs_to :customer    # there's a column "customer_id" in the db table
end

def LineItem < ActiveRecord::Base
  belongs_to :order # there's a column "order_id" in the db table
end

def Customer < ActiveRecord::Base
  has_many :orders
  has_one :address
end
```

```
def Address < ActiveRecord::Base
  belongs_to :customer
end

belongs_to  :some_model,
        :class_name  => 'MyClass',      # specifies other class name
        :foreign_key => 'my_real_id',   # and primary key
        :conditions  => 'column = 0'    # only finds when this condition met

has_one :some_model,
        # as belongs_to and additionally:
        :dependent  => :destroy         # deletes associated object
        :order      => 'name ASC'       # SQL fragment for sorting

has_many :some_model
        # as has_one and additionally:
        :dependent => :destroy          # deletes all dependent data
                                        # calling each objects destroy

        :dependent => :delete_all       # deletes all dependent data
                                        # without calling the destroy methods

        :dependent => :nullify          # set association to null, not
                                        # destroying objects

        :group => 'name'                # adds GROUP BY fragment
        :finder_sql => 'select ....'    # instead of the Rails finders
        :counter_sql => 'select ...'    # instead of the Rails counters
def Category < ActiveRecord::Base
  has_and_belongs_to_many :products
end
def Product < ActiveRecord::Base
  has_and_belongs_to_many :categories
end
```

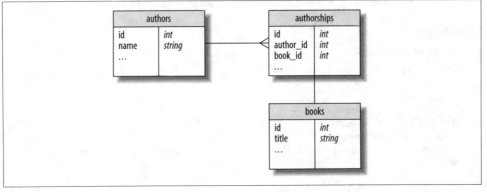

*Figure B-1. One-to-one and one-to-many relationships*

Table categories_products:

- Has category_id column
- Has product_id column
- Does not have id column

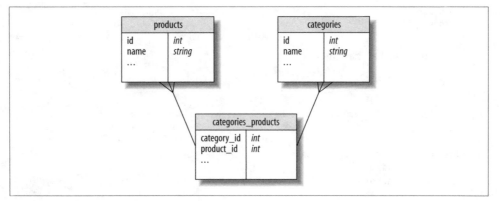

*Figure B-2. Many-to-many relationships*

## Association Join Models (Figure B-3)

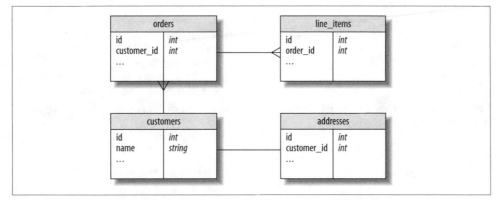

*Figure B-3. Through model*

```
class Author < ActiveRecord::Base
  has_many :authorships
  has_many :books, :through => :authorships
end

class Authorship < ActiveRecord::Base
  belongs_to :author
  belongs_to :book
end

class Book < ActiveRecord::Base
  has_one :authorship
end

@author = Author.find :first
@author.authorships.collect { |a| a.book } # selects all books that the author's
                                            # authorships belong to.
```

```
@author.books                          # selects all books by using the
Authorship
                                       # join model
```

Also works through has_many associations:

```
class Firm < ActiveRecord::Base
  has_many    :clients
  has_many    :invoices, :through => :clients
  has_many    :paid_invoices, :through => :clients, :source => :invoice
end

class Client < ActiveRecord::Base
  belongs_to :firm
  has_many    :invoices
end

class Invoice < ActiveRecord::Base
  belongs_to :client
end

@firm = Firm.find :first
@firm.clients.collect { |c| c.invoices }.flatten # select all invoices for all
clients
                                       # of the firm
@firm.invoices                         # selects all invoices by going
                                       # through the Client join model.
```

Learn more at the following address: *http://api.rubyonrails.com/classes/ActiveRecord/
Associations/ClassMethods.html.*

## Validations

```
validates_presence_of :firstname, :lastname    # must be filled out

validates_length_of :password,
                    :minimum => 8          # more than 8 characters
                    :maximum => 16         # shorter than 16 characters
                    :in => 8..16           # between 8 and 16 characters
                    :too_short => 'way too short'
                    :too_long => 'way to long'

validates_acceptance_of :eula             # Must accept a condition
                    :accept => 'Y'         # default: 1 (ideal for a checkbox)

validates_confirmation_of :password
# the fields password and password_confirmation must match

validates_uniqueness_of :user_name                # user_name has to be unique
                    :scope => 'account_id'  # Condition:
                                            # account_id = user.account_id

validates_format_of :email          # field must match a regular expression
                    :with => /^(+)@((?:[-a-z0-9]+/.)+[a-z]{2,})$/i

validates_numericality_of   :value                # value is numeric
```

```
                          :only_integer => true
                          :allow_nil => true

     validates_inclusion_in  :gender,      # value is in enumeration
                             :in => %w( m, f )

     validates_exclusion_of  :age            # value is not in Enumeration
                             :in => 13..19    # don't want any teenagers

     validates_associated :relation
     # validates that the associated object is valid
```

Validation options:

```
     :message => 'my own errormessage'
     :on      => :create               # or :update (validates only then)
     :if      => ...                   # call method oder Proc
```

Learn more: *http://api.rubyonrails.com/classes/ActiveRecord/Validations.html*.

## Calculations

```
     Person.average :age
     Person.minimum :age
     Person.maximum :age
     Person.count
     Person.count(:conditions => "age > 26")
     Person.sum :salary, :group => :last_name
```

Learn more at the following address: *http://api.rubyonrails.com/classes/ActiveRecord/Calculations/ClassMethods.html*.

## Finders

```
     find(42)                           # object with ID 42
     find([37, 42])                     # Array with the objects with id 37, 42
     find :all
     find :first,
         :conditions => [ "name = ?", "Hans" ]  # finds the first record
                                                 # with matching condition
```

More parameters for find:

```
     :order => 'name DESC'          # sql fragment for sorting
     :offset => 20                  # starts with entry 20
     :limit => 10                   # only return 10 objects
     :group => 'name'               # sql fragment GROUP BY
     :joins => 'LEFT JOIN ...'      # additional LEFT JOIN (rarely used)
     :include => [:account, :friends]    # LEFT OUTER JOIN with these model
     :include => { :groups => { :members=> { :favorites } } }
     :select => [:name, :adress]    # instead of SELECT * FROM
     :readonly => true              # objects are write protected
```

### Dynamic attribute-based finders

```
     Person.find_by_user_name(user_name)
     Person.find_all_by_last_name(last_name)
     Person.find_by_user_name_and_password(user_name, password)
     Order.find_by_name("Joe Blow")
```

```
      Order.find_by_email("jb@gmail.com")
      Slideshow.find_or_create_by_name("Winter")
```
Learn more: *http://api.rubyonrails.com/classes/ActiveRecord/Base.html*.

### Scope

```
    Employee.with_scope(
       :find => { :conditions => "salary > 10000",
                  :limit => 10 }) do
    Employee.find(:all)     # => SELECT * FROM employees
                            #              WHERE (salary > 10000)
                            #              LIMIT 10

      # scope is cumulative
      Employee.with_scope(
        :find => { :conditions => "name = 'Jamis'" }) do
        Employee.find(:all)    # => SELECT * FROM employees
                               #              WHERE ( salary > 10000 )
                               #              AND ( name = 'Jamis' ))
                               #              LIMIT 10
      end

      # all previous scope is ignored
      Employee.with_exclusive_scope(
        :find => { :conditions => "name = 'Jamis'" }) do
        Employee.find(:all)    # => SELECT * FROM employees
                               #              WHERE (name = 'Jamis')
      end
    end
```
Learn more:

- *http://www.codyfauser.com/articles/2006/02/01/using-with_scope-to-refactor-messy-finders*
- *http://blog.caboo.se/articles/2006/02/22/nested-with_scope*

### Acts

acts_as_list:

```
    class TodoList < ActiveRecord::Base
       has_many :todo_items, :order => "position"
    end

    class TodoItem < ActiveRecord::Base
      belongs_to :todo_list
      acts_as_list :scope => :todo_list
    end

    todo_list.first.move_to_bottom
    todo_list.last.move_higher
```
Learn more:

- *http://api.rubyonrails.com/classes/ActiveRecord/Acts/List/ClassMethods.html*
- *http://api.rubyonrails.com/classes/ActiveRecord/Acts/List/InstanceMethods.html*

```
acts_as_tree:
    class Category < ActiveRecord::Base
       acts_as_tree :order => "name"
    end

    Example :
    root
     /_ child1
           /_ subchild1
           /_ subchild2

    root      = Category.create("name" => "root")
    child1    = root.children.create("name" => "child1")
    subchild1 = child1.children.create("name" => "subchild1")

    root.parent    # => nil
    child1.parent # => root
    root.children # => [child1]
    root.children.first.children.first # => subchild1
```

Learn more: *http://api.rubyonrails.com/classes/ActiveRecord/Acts/Tree/ClassMethods.html.*

## Callbacks

Callbacks are hooks into the life cycle of an Active Record object that allows you to trigger logic before or after an alteration of the object state (Table B-1).

*Table B-1. Active Record object life cycle*

| Object state | Callback |
| --- | --- |
| save | |
| valid? | |
| | before_validation |
| | before_validation_on_create |
| validate | |
| validate_on_create | |
| | after_validation |
| | after_validation_on_create |
| | before_save |
| | before_create |
| create | |
| | after_create |
| | after_save |

Example:

```
class Subscription < ActiveRecord::Base
  before_create :record_signup
private
  def record_signup
```

```
      self.signed_up_on = Date.today
    end
  end

  class Firm < ActiveRecord::Base
    # Destroys the associated clients and people when the firm is destroyed
    before_destroy { |record| Person.destroy_all "firm_id = #{record.id}"   }
    before_destroy { |record| Client.destroy_all "client_of = #{record.id}" }
  end
```

Learn more: *http://api.rubyonrails.com/classes/ActiveRecord/Callbacks.html*.

## Observers

The Observer classes let you extract the functionality of the callbacks:

```
  class CommentObserver < ActiveRecord::Observer
    def after_save(comment)
      Notifications.deliver_comment("admin@do.com", "New comment was posted", comment)
    end
  end
```

- Store observers in *app/model/model_observer.rb*.
- Enable observer by putting this in *config/environment.rb*:

```
      config.active_record.observers = :comment_observer, :signup_observer
```

Learn more: *http://api.rubyonrails.com/classes/ActiveRecord/Observer.html*.

## Migration

```
  > ruby script/generate migration MyAddTables
```

Creates the file *db/migrations/001_my_add_tables.rb*. The methods up( ) and down( ) change
the db schema:

```
  def self.up      # brings db schema to the next version
    create_table :table, :force => true do |t|
      t.column :name, :string
      t.column :age, :integer, { :default => 42 }
      t.column :description, :text
      # :string, :text, :integer, :float, :datetime, :timestamp, :time, :date,
      # :binary, :boolean
    end
    add_column :table, :column, :type
    rename_column :table, :old_name, :new_name
    change_column :table, :column, :new_type
    execute "SQL Statement"
    add_index :table, :column, :unique => true, :name => 'some_name'
    add_index :table, [ :column1, :column2 ]
  end

  def self.down    # rollbacks changes
    rename_column :table, :new_name, :old_name
    remove_column :table, :column
    drop_table :table
    remove_index :table, :column
  end
```

To execute the migration:

```
> rake db:migrate
> rake db:migrate VERSION=14
> rake db:migrate RAILS_ENV=production
```

Learn more:

- *http://api.rubyonrails.org/classes/ActiveRecord/Migration.html*
- *http://glu.ttono.us/articles/2005/10/27/the-joy-of-migrations*
- *http://jamis.jamisbuck.org/articles/2005/09/27/getting-started-with-activerecord-migrations*

# Controllers

## Controller Methods

Each public method in a controller is callable by the default URL scheme */controller/action* (/world/hello, in this example):

```
class WorldController < ApplicationController
def hello
  render :text => 'Hello world'
end
```

All request parameters, whether they come from a GET or POST request, or from the URL, are available through the params hash:

```
/world/hello/1?foo=bar
id = params[:id]     # 1
foo = params[:foo]   # bar
```

Instance variables defined in the controller's methods are available to the corresponding view templates:

```
def show
  @person = Person.find( params[:id])
end
```

Determine the type of response accepted:

```
def index
  @posts = Post.find :all

  respond_to do |type|
    type.html # using defaults, which will render weblog/index.rhtml
    type.xml  { render :action => "index.rxml" }
    type.js   { render :action => "index.rjs" }
  end
end
```

Learn more: *http://api.rubyonrails.com/classes/ActionController/Base.html*.

## Render

Usually the view template with the same name as the controller method is used to render the results.

### Action

```
render :action => 'some_action'    # the default. Does not need to be specified
                                   # in a controller method called "some_action"
render :action => 'another_action', :layout => false
render :action => 'some_action', :layout => 'another_layout'
```

### Partials

Partials are stored in files whose filename begins with an underscore (like _error, _subform, and _listitem):

```
render :partial => 'subform'
render :partial => 'error', :status => 500
render :partial => 'subform', :locals => { :variable => @other_variable }
render :partial => 'listitem', :collection => @list
render :partial => 'listitem', :collection => @list, :spacer_template => 'list_
divider'
```

### Templates

Similar to rendering an action, but finds the template based on the template root (*app/ views*):

```
render :template => 'weblog/show'   # renders app/views/weblog/show
```

### Files

```
render :file => '/path/to/some/file.rhtml'
render :file => '/path/to/some/filenotfound.rhtml', status => 404, :layout => true
```

### Text

```
render :text => "Hello World"
render :text => "This is an error", :status => 500
render :text => "Let's use a layout", :layout => true
render :text => 'Specific layout', :layout => 'special'
```

### Inline Template

Uses ERb to render the "miniature" template:

```
render :inline => "<%= 'hello , ' * 3 + 'again' %>"
render :inline => "<%= 'hello ' + name %>", :locals => { :name => "david" }
```

### RJS

```
def refresh
  render :update do |page|
    page.replace_html 'user_list', :partial => 'user', :collection => @users
    page.visual_effect :highlight, 'user_list'
  end
end
```

### Change content_type

```
render :action => "atom.rxml", :content_type => "application/atom+xml"
```

### Redirects

```
redirect_to(:action => "edit")
redirect_to(:controller => "accounts", :action => "signup")
```

### Nothing

```
render :nothing
render :nothing, :status => 403     # forbidden
```

Learn more:

- *http://api.rubyonrails.com/classes/ActionView/Base.html*
- *http://api.rubyonrails.com/classes/ActionController/Base.html*

### URL Routing

In *config/routes.rb*:

```
map.connect '', :controller => 'posts', :action => 'list' # default
map.connect ':action/:controller/:id'
map.connect 'tasks/:year/:month', :controller => 'tasks',
                                  :action => 'by_date',
                                  :month => nil, :year => nil,
                                  :requirements => {:year => //d{4}/,
                                                    :month => //d{1,2}/ }
```

Learn more: *http://manuals.rubyonrails.com/read/chapter/65*.

### Filter

Filters can change a request before or after the controller. They can, for example, be used for authentication, encryption, or compression:

```
before_filter :login_required, :except => [ :login ]
before_filter :autenticate, :only => [ :edit, :delete ]
after_filter :compress
```

It's also possible to use a proc for a really small filter action:

```
before_filter { |controller| false if controller.params["stop_action"] }
```

Change the order of your filters by using prepend_before_filter and prepend_after_filter (like prepend_before_filter :some_filter, which will put the some_filter at the beginning of the filter chain).

If you define a filter in a superclass, you can skip it in the subclass:

```
skip_before_filter :some_filter
skip_after_filter :some_filter
```

Learn more: *http://api.rubyonrails.com/classes/ActionController/Filters/ClassMethods.html*.

## Session/Flash

To save data across multiple requests, you can use either the session or the flash hashes. A flash stores a value (normally text) until the next request, while a session stores data during the complete session.

```
session[:user] = @user
flash[:message] = "Data was saved successfully"

<%= link_to "login", :action => 'login' unless session[:user] %>
<% if flash[:message] %>
<div><%= h flash[:message] %></div>
<% end %>
```

### Session management

It's possible to turn off session management:

```
session :off                          # turn session managment off
session :off, :only => :action        # only for this :action
session :off, :except => :action      # except for this action
session :only => :foo,                # only for :foo when doing HTTPS
        :session_secure => true
session :off, :only => :foo,          # off for foo, if uses as Web Service
        :if => Proc.new { |req| req.parameters[:ws] }
```

Learn more at the following site: *http://api.rubyonrails.com/classes/ActionController/ SessionManagement/ClassMethods.html*.

## Cookies

### Setting

```
cookies[:user_name] = "david" # => Will set a simple session cookie
cookies[:login] = { :value => "XJ-122", :expires => Time.now + 3600}
    # => Will set a cookie that expires in 1 hour
```

### Reading

```
cookies[:user_name] # => "david"
cookies.size        # => 2
```

### Deleting

```
cookies.delete :user_name
```

Option symbols for setting cookies:

*value*
> The cookie's value or list of values (as an array).

*path*
> The path for which this cookie applies (defaults to the root of the application).

*domain*
> The domain for which this cookie applies.

*expires*
> The time at which this cookie expires, as a Time object.

*secure*
>    Whether this cookie is a secure cookie (defaults to false). Secure cookies are trans-
>    mitted only to HTTPS servers.

Learn more: *http://api.rubyonrails.com/classes/ActionController/Cookies.html*.

## Views

### View Templates

All view templates are stored in *app/views/controllername*. The extension determines what
kind of template it is:

`*.rhtml`
>    Ruby HTML (using ERB)

`*.rxml`
>    Ruby XML (using Builder)

`*.rjs`
>    Ruby JavaScript

All instance variables of the controller are available to the view. In addition, the following
special objects can be accessed:

`headers`
>    The headers of the outgoing response

`request`
>    The incoming request object

`response`
>    The outgoing response object

`params`
>    The parameter hash

`session`
>    The session hash

`controller`
>    The current controller

### RHTML

RHTML is HTML mixed with Ruby, using tags. All of Ruby is available for programming:

```
<% %>    # executes the Ruby code
<%= %>   # executes the Ruby code and displays the result

<ul>
<% @products.each do |p| %>
  <li><%= h @p.name %></li>
<% end %>
</ul>
```

The output of anything in <%= %> tags is directly copied to the HTML output stream. To secure against HTML injection, use the h( ) function to HTML-escape the output. For example:

```
<%=h @user_entered_notes %>
```

## RXML

Creates XML files:

```
xml.instruct!                    # <?xml version="1.0" encoding="UTF-8"?>
xml.comment! "a comment"         # <!-- a comment -->
xml.feed "xmlns" => "http://www.w3.org/2005/Atom" do
  xml.title "My Atom Feed"
  xml.subtitle h(@feed.subtitle), "type" => 'html'
  xml.link url_for( :only_path => false,
                    :controller => 'feed',
                    :action => 'atom' )
  xml.updated @updated.iso8601
  xml.author do
    xml.name "Jens-Christian Fischer"
    xml.email "jcfischer@gmail.com"
  end
  @entries.each do |entry|
    xml.entry do
      xml.title entry.title
      xml.link "href" => url_for ( :only_path => false,
                                   :controller => 'entries',
                                   :action => 'show',
                                   :id => entry )

      xml.id entry.urn
      xml.updated entry.updated.iso8601
      xml.summary h(entry.summary)
    end
  end
end
```

Learn more: *http://rubyforge.org/projects/builder/*.

## RJS

In addition to HTML and XML templates, Rails also understands JavaScript templates. They allow you to easily create complex alterations of the displayed page. You can manipulate a page element with the following methods:

select

Select a DOM element for further processing:

```
page.select('pattern') # selects an item on the page through a CSS pattern
                       # select('p'), select('p.welcome b')
page.select('div.header em').first.hide
page.select('#items li').eacj do |value|
  value.hide
end
```

insert_html
> Inserts content into the DOM at a specific position:
>
>     page.insert_html :position, id, content
>
> position can be one of the following:
>
>     :top
>     :bottom
>     :before
>     :after

replace_html
> Replaces the inner HTML of the specified DOM element:
>
>     page.replace_html 'title', "This is the new title"
>     page.replace_html 'person-45', :partial => 'person', :object => @person

replace
> Replaces the outer HTML (i.e., the entire element) of the specified DOM element:
>
>     page.replace 'task', :partial => 'task', :object => @task

remove
> Removes the specified DOM element:
>
>     page.remove 'edit-button'

hide
> Hides the specified DOM element:
>
>     page.hide 'some-element'

show
> Shows the specified DOM element:
>
>     page.show 'some-element'

toggle
> Toggles the visibility of a DOM element:
>
>     page.toggle 'some-element'

alert
> Displays an alert box:
>
>     page.alert 'Hello world'

redirect_to
> Redirects the browser to a given location:
>
>     page.redirect_to :controller => 'blog', :action => 'show', :id => @post

call
> Calls another JavaScript function:
>
>     page.call foo, 1, 2

assign
> Assigns a value to a JavaScript variable:
>
>     page.assign "foo", 42

<<
> Writes raw JavaScript to the page:
>
>     page << "alert('hello world);"

delay
>    Delays the code in the block by a number of seconds:

```
page.delay(10) do
    page.visual_effect :fade, 'notice'
end
```

visual_effect
>    Calls a Scriptaculous effect:

```
page.visual_effect :highlight, 'notice', :duration => 2
```

sortable
>    Creates a sortable element:

```
page.sortable 'my_list', :url => { :action => 'order' }
```

dragable
>    Creates a draggable element:

```
page.dragable 'my_image', :revert => true
```

drop_receiving
>    Creates an element for receiving drops:

```
page.drop_recieving 'my_cart', :url => { :controller => 'cart',
                                         :action => 'add' }
```

Learn more: *http://api.rubyonrails.com/classes/ActionView/Base.html*.

## Helpers

Small functions, normally used for displaying data, can be extracted to helpers. Each view has its own helper class (in *app/helpers*). Common functionality is stored in *app/helpers/ application_helper.rb*.

## Links

```
link_to "Name", :controller => 'post', :action => 'show', :id => @post.id
link_to "Delete", { :controller => "admin",
  :action => "delete",
  :id => @post },
{ :class => 'css-class',
  :id => 'css-id',
  :confirm => "Are you sure?" }

image_tag "spinner.png", :class => "image", :alt => "Spinner"

mail_to "info@invisible.ch", "send mail",
      :subject => "Support request by #{@user.name}",
        :cc => @user.email,
        :body => '....',
        :encoding => "javascript"

stylesheet_link_tag "scaffold", "admin", :media => "all"
```

Learn more: *http://api.rubyonrails.com/classes/ActionView/Helpers/UrlHelper.html*.

## HTML Forms

### Form

```
<%= form_tag { :action => :save }, { :method => :post } %>
```

This creates a form tag with the specified action, and makes it a POST request.

Use :multipart => true to define a MIME-multipart form (for file uploads).

### Text Fields

```
<%= text_field :modelname, :attribute_name, options %>
```

The following creates a text input field of the form:

```
<input type="text" name="modelname[attribute_name]" id="attributename" />
```

Example:

```
text_field "post", "title", "size" => 20
    <input  type="text" id="post_title" name="post[title]"
            size="20" value="#{@post.title}" />
```

Create a hidden field:

```
<%= hidden_field ... %>
```

Create a password field (all input shown as stars):

```
<%= password_field ... %>
```

Create a file field:

```
<%= file_field ... %>
```

### Text Area

```
<%= text_area ... %>
```

This example:

```
text_area "post", "body", "cols" => 20, "rows" => 40
```

generates:

```
<textarea cols="20" rows="40" id="post_body" name="post[body]">
    #{@post.body}
</textarea>
```

### Radio Button

```
<%= radio_button :modelname, :attribute, :tag_value, options %>
```

Example:

```
radio_button "post", "category", "rails"
radio_button "post", "category", "java"
    <input type="radio" id="post_category" name="post[category]" value="rails"
        checked="checked" />
    <input type="radio" id="post_category" name="post[category]" value="java" />
```

### Checkbox

```
<%= check_box :modelname, :attribute, options, on_value, off_value %>
```

Example:

```
check_box "post", "validated"   # post.validated? returns 1 or 0
    <input type="checkbox" id="post_validate" name="post[validated]"
```

```
                  value="1" checked="checked" />
        <input name="post[validated]" type="hidden" value="0" />

    check_box "puppy", "gooddog", {}, "yes", "no"
        <input type="checkbox" id="puppy_gooddog" name="puppy[gooddog]" value="yes" />
        <input name="puppy[gooddog]" type="hidden" value="no" />
```

## Options

Creates a select tag. Pass an array of choices:

```
<%= select :variable, :attribute, choices, options, html_options %>
```

Example:

```
select    "post",
          "person_id",
          Person.find_all.collect {|p| [ p.name, p.id ] },
          { :include_blank => true }

  <select name="post[person_id]">
    <option></option>
    <option value="1" selected="selected">David</option>
    <option value="2">Sam</option>
    <option value="3">Tobias</option>
  </select>

<%= collection_select :variable, :attribute, choices, :id, :value %>
```

## Date and Time

```
<%= date_select :variable, :attribute, options %>
<%= datetime_select :variable, :attribute, options %>
```

Examples:

```
date_select "post", "written_on"
date_select "user", "birthday", :start_year => 1910
date_select "user", "cc_date", :start_year => 2005,
                               :use_month_numbers => true,
                               :discard_day => true,
                               :order => [:year, :month]

datetime_select "post", "written_on"
```

## end_form Tag

```
<%= end_form_tag %>
```

Learn more: *http://api.rubyonrails.com/classes/ActionView/Helpers/FormHelper.html*.

## Layouts

A layout defines the surroundings of an HTML page. You use it to define common look and feel. Layouts live in *app/views/layouts*:

```
<html>
  <head>
    <title>Form: <%= controller.action_name %></title>
    <%= stylesheet_link_tag 'scaffold' %>
  </head>
```

```
    <body>
      <%= yield %>    # the content will show up here
    </body>
</html>
----
class MyController < ApplicationController
  layout "standard", :except => [ :rss, :atom ]
...
end
----
class MyOtherController < ApplicationController
  layout :compute_layout

  # this method computes the name of the layout to use
  def compute_layout
    return "admin" if session[:role] == "admin"
    "standard"
  end
  ...
end
```

Layouts have access to the instance variables of the controller.

Learn more: *http://api.rubyonrails.com/classes/ActionController/Layout/ClassMethods.html*.

## Partials

Partials are building blocks for creating views. They allow you to reuse commonly used display blocks. They are stored in files:

```
render :partial => 'product'
```

This command loads the partial in *_product.rthml* and passes the instance variable @product to it. The partial can access it using @product:

```
render :partial => 'product', :locals => { :product => @bought }
```

This command loads the same partial but assigns a different instance variable to it:

```
render :partial => 'product', :collection => @product_list
```

This renders the partial for each element in @product_list and assigns @product to each element. An iteration counter is automatically made available to the template with a name of the form partial_name_counter (in the previous example, product_counter).

Learn more: *http://api.rubyonrails.com/classes/ActionView/Partials.html*.

## Ajax

Be sure to include the JavaScript libraries in the layout:

```
<%= javascript_include_tag :defaults %>
```

### Linking to Remote Action

```
<%= link_to_remote "link", :update => 'some_div',
                         :url => { :action => 'show', :id => post.id } %>

<%= link_to_remote "link", :url => { :action => 'create',
```

```
                       :update => { :success => 'good_div',
                                    :failure => 'error_div' },
                       :loading => 'Element.show('spinner'),
                       :complete => 'Element.hide('spinner') } %>
```

## Callbacks

:loading
> Called when the remote document is being loaded with data by the browser.

:loaded
> Called when the browser has finished loading the remote document.

:interactive
> Called when the user can interact with the remote document, even though it has not finished loading.

:success
> Called when the XMLHttpRequest is completed, and the HTTP status code is in the 2XX range.

:failure
> Called when the XMLHttpRequest is completed, and the HTTP status code is not in the 2XX range.

:complete
> Called when the XMLHttpRequest is complete (fires after success/failure if they are present).

You can also specify reactions to return codes directly:

```
link_to_remote word,
    :url => { :action => "action" },
    404 => "alert('Not found...? Wrong URL...?')",
    :failure => "alert('HTTP Error ' + request.status + '!')"
```

## Ajax Forms

You can create a form that will submit via an XMLHttpRequest instead of a POST request. The parameters are passed exactly the same way (so the controller can use the params method to access the parameters). Fallback for non-JavaScript-enabled browsers can be specified by using the :action methods in the :html option:

```
form_remote_tag :html => { :action => url_for(:controller => 'controller',
                                               :action => 'action'),
                           :method => :post }
```

## Autocompleting Text Field

In the view t\emplate:

```
<%= text_field_with_auto_complete :model, :attribute %>
```

In the controller:

```
auto_complete_for :model, :attribute
```

### Observe Field

```
<label for="search">Search term:</label>
<%= text_field_tag :search %>
<%= observe_field(:search,
                  :frequency => 0.5,
                  :update => :results,
                  :url => { :action => :search }) %>
<div id="results"></div>
```

Optionally specify:

```
:on => :blur    # trigger for event (default :changed or :clicked)
:with => ...    # a JavaScript expression to specify what value is sent
                # defaults to "value"
:with => 'bla'  # "'bla' = value"
:with => 'a=b'  # "a=b"
```

### Observe Form

Same semantics as observe_field.

### periodically_call_remote

```
<%= periodically_call_remote(:update => 'process-list',
                             :url => { :action => :ps },
                             :frequency => 2 ) %>
```

Learn more: *http://api.rubyonrails.com/classes/ActionView/Helpers/JavaScriptHelper.html.*

## Configuring Your Application

A lot of things can be configured in the *config/environment.rb* file. This list is not exhaustive:

### Session Configuration

```
config.action_controller.session_store = :active_record_store
# one of :active_record_store, :drb_store,
# :mem_cache_store, or :memory_store or your own class

ActionController::Base.session_options[:session_key] = 'my_app'
    # use an application specific session_key
ActionController::Base.session_options[:session_id] = '12345'
    # use this session_id. Will be created if not specified
ActionController::Base.session_options[:session_expires] = 3.minute.from_now
    # how long before a session expires?
ActionController::Base.session_options[:new_session] = true
    # force the creation of a new session
ActionController::Base.session_options[:session_secure] = true
    # only use sessions over HTTPS
ActionController::Base.session_options[:session_domain] = 'invisible.ch'
    # Specify which domain this session is valid for (default: hostname of server)
ActionController::Base.session_options[:session_path] = '/my_app'
    # the path for which this session applies.  Defaults to the
    # directory of the CGI script
```

Learn more at the following address: *http://api.rubyonrails.com/classes/ActionController/ SessionManagement/ClassMethods.html*.

## Caching Configuration

```
ActionController::Base.fragment_cache_store = :file_store, "/path/to/cache/directory"
```

Learn more: *http://api.rubyonrails.com/classes/ActionController/Caching.html*.

# Index

We'd like to hear your suggestions for improving our indexes. Send email to *index@oreilly.com*.

## C

categories, 78
  assigning, 81
categories_controller.rb, 79
Category model class, 108
Category.find method, 83
category.rb, 79, 108
change_filter method, 108
collect method, 83
collection_select helper, 107
collection_select method, 81
columns, 27
commercial IDEs for Rails, 135
components, 5
concurrency management, optimistic
        locking, 52
config/routes.rb, 75
controllers, 10–13
  Action Pack framework, 11
  code generated by Rails, 60–63
  creating, 10
  index action, 12
  layouts and, 73
  quick reference, 149–153
  running, 10
  tying to views, 15
create method, 83
CSS (Cascading Stylesheets), 75
  application.css, 75
  photo.css, 76
  scaffold.css, 75
  slideshows.css, 88, 97, 106

## D

databases, 37
databases supported by Rails, 135
Development environment, Rails, 23
directories, 5
dispatcher, 12
div tags, 86
documentation, 134
domain-specific language (DSL), 20
draggable_element helper, 103
drop_receiving_element helper, 103
DSL (domain-specific language), 20

## E

each_with_index, 97
Eclipse, 132
edit app/views/photos/list.rhtml, 77
edit method, 82, 83

edit.rhtml, 95, 100, 107
editors, 135
environments, 114
expressions, 15

## F

finders, 33
fixtures, 116
foreign keys, 37
_form.rhtml, 81
Fowler, Martin, 2, 18
functional tests, 114, 119–124

## G

gems, 3
generate scripts, 10
generators, 11
  quick reference, 140

## H

has_and_belongs_to_many, 44–47
has_many, 40–43
  metaprogramming, 42
has_one, 43
  metaprogramming, 40
helper functions, 87
hierarchical categories, 78
HTML
  forms, 157–158
    check boxes, 157
    date and time, 158
    end_form tag, 158
    form tag, 157
    options, 158
    radio buttons, 157
    text areas, 157
    text fields, 157
  fragments, 92
  helper functions for, 87
  mixed with Ruby, 153
  multiple-selection list boxes, 82
  page layouts, 72, 74, 158
  stylesheets, advantages of, 75
  templates and ERb, 68

## I

identifiers, 28
IDEs (integrated development environments)
        for Rails, 135
image_tag helper, 103

photos/app/views/slideshows/edit.rhtml, 95,
  100, 107
photos/public/stylesheets/slideshows.css,
  97, 106
photos_controller.rb, 82
plugins, quick references, 140
primary keys, 37
Production environment, Rails, 23
Prototype library, 92
public/stylesheets/photos.css, 76
public/stylesheets/slideshows.css, 88

# R

RadRails, 130, 132
Rails, 1, 21
    advantages, 2
    Ajax implementation, 91
    debugging resources, 136
    directories, 5
    editors, 135
    environments, 3, 23
    generators, 11
    IDEs (integrated development
        environments), 135
    installation via gems, 3
    installing, 129–133
        Instant Rails, 129
        Linux, 133
        Locomotive on OS X, 131
        OS X, 131
        RadRails, 130
        Windows installations, 129–131
    JavaScript files, 95
    Production environment, 23
    quick reference, 134–162
        Active Record, 141–149
        Ajax, 159–161
        applications, creating, 136
        controllers, 149–153
        documentation, 134
        generators, 140
        plug-ins, 140
        Rails applications, configuring, 161
        rake, 138
        RJS (Ruby JavaScript), 140
        scripts, 139
        testing, 136–138
        views, 153–159
    supported databases, 135
    supported web servers, 135
    test environment, 23
    testing (see testing)

Rails JavaScript templates, 154
rake, 138
rapid feedback loop, 12
relational databases, 37
relationship tables, 44
relationships, 36
    acts_as_list, 47–50
    belongs_to, 37–40
    has_and_belongs_to_many, 44–47
    has_many, 40–43
    has_one, 43
    trees, 50–52
remove_slide method, 105
render_scaffold method, 57
request scopes, 17
requests, 65
RHTML
    quick reference, 153
RJS (Ruby JavaScript), 140
RJS quick refernce, 154
routes.rb, 75
Ruby
    gems, 3
Ruby JavaScript (RJS), 140
ruby keyword, 6
ruby script/generate scaffold command, 60
RubyDoc, 5

# S

scaffold.css, 75
scaffolding, 2, 54–64
    advantages, 54
    code generation, 60–63
    controller names, pluralization, 61
    limitations, 64
    relationships and, 95
    render_scaffold method, 57
    replacing, 57
    scaffold :photo method, 55
    scaffold method, 54–57
        scaffold :target method, 56
schema migrations (see migrations)
script.aculo.us library, 92
script/generate script, 11
script/server script, 7
    defaults, 7
scriptlets, 15
scripts, 139
Selenium, 126
server requests, 65
sessions, 92
show.rhtml, 93

## About the Authors

**Bruce A. Tate** is a kayaker, mountain biker, and father of two from Austin, Texas. In 2001, he founded the J2Life, LLC independent consultancy—now called RapidRed—where his primary focus is on training, implementation, and consulting for rapid software development using Ruby on Rails. His customers have included FedEx, Great West Life, AutoGas, TheServerSide, and BEA. His 20 years of experience span a 13-year stint at IBM and several leadership positions at various startup companies. He's an international speaker and widely respected author of nine software development books, including the provocative *Beyond Java* (O'Reilly), the Jolt-winning *Better, Faster, Lighter Java* (O'Reilly), the management-focused *From Java to Ruby* (Pragmatic), and the smash hit *Bitter Java* (Manning).

**Curt Hibbs** has always been slightly obsessed with new technologies and tracking technology trends. But he will tell you that this is simply because he is lazy, always looking for new methods and technologies to make his work easier and more productive. This tendency led to his discovery of Ruby in 2001 (when it was still relatively unknown outside of Japan) and to his founding several highly successful Ruby open source projects. For most of his professional career, which started in the early 1970s, Curt has been a consultant to well-known companies such as Hewlett Packard, Intuit, Corel, WordStar, Charles Schwab, Vivendi Universal, and more. He has also been a principal in several startups. Curt now works as a Senior Software Engineer for The Boeing Company in St. Louis.

## Colophon

The animal on the cover of *Ruby on Rails: Up and Running* is an ibex (*Capra pyrenaica*). Found in the mountains of Europe, central Asia, and North Africa, the ibex spends most of its time at an altitude of 7,500 to 11,500 feet. The ibex is known for its impressively long horns, which can grow up to three feet on males. During mating season, ibex males bang their horns together in intense battles over mating rights.

Although the physics of such a feat seems dubious, according to legend, the ibex's horns were so strong that, if threatened, the animal could hurl itself from a precipice and land unharmed on them.

The cover image is from *Riverside Natural History*. The cover font is Adobe ITC Garamond. The text font is Linotype Birka; the heading font is Adobe Myriad Condensed; and the code font is LucasFont's TheSans Mono Condensed.

# Better than e-books

**Buy *Ruby on Rails: Up and Running* and access the digital edition FREE on Safari for 45 days.**

Go to www.oreilly.com/go/safarienabled
and type in coupon code LGN9-NLWL-5MSU-NFLS-3YX5

**Search**
thousands of
top tech books

**Download**
whole chapters

**Cut and Paste**
code examples

**Find**
answers fast

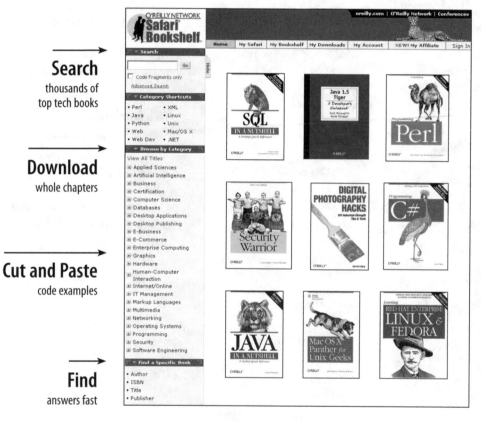

Search Safari! The premier electronic reference
library for programmers and IT professionals.

# Related Titles from O'Reilly

## Web Programming

ActionScript 3 Cookbook

ActionScript for Flash MX: The Definitive Guide, *2nd Edition*

Ajax Hacks

Dynamic HTML: The Definitive Reference, *2nd Edition*

Flash Hacks

Essential PHP Security

Google Advertising Tools

Google Hacks, *2nd Edition*

Google Map Hacks

Google Pocket Guide

Google: The Missing Manual, *2nd Edition*

Head First HTML with CSS & XHTML

Head Rush Ajax

HTTP: The Definitive Guide

JavaScript & DHTML Cookbook

JavaScript Pocket Reference, *2nd Edition*

JavaScript: The Definitive Guide, *4th Edition*

Learning PHP 5

Learning PHP and MySQL

PHP Cookbook

PHP Hacks

PHP in a Nutshell

PHP Pocket Reference, *2nd Edition*

PHPUnit Pocket Guide

Programming ColdFusion MX, *2nd Edition*

Programming PHP, *2nd Edition*

Upgrading to PHP 5

Web Database Applications with PHP and MySQL, *2nd Edition*

Web Site Cookbook

Webmaster in a Nutshell, *3rd Edition*

## Web Administration

Apache Cookbook

Apache Pocket Reference

Apache: The Definitive Guide, *3rd Edition*

Perl for Web Site Management

Squid: The Definitive Guide

Web Performance Tuning, *2nd Edition*